ESSAY I:

THE TYRANNY OF RATIONALITY

CHAPTER I

THE BIRTH OF REASON AND THE DEATH OF TRAGEDY

"Reason. How did reason come into the world? As is fitting, in an irrational manner. One will have to guess at it as at a riddle."

Friedrich Nietzsche

In attempting to come to an understanding of the origin of reason and its significance for the Western intellect, attention shall be directed to the period in the history of the Western mind in which reason arose to become the dominant intellectual influence. In looking for aid in this discussion, many of the works, aphorisms, and fragments of the Nietzsche corpus are germaine. Nietzsche, both as a philologist and as a philosopher, dealt with this problem with seriousness, imagination, and scholarly sophistication, as will become evident from a discussion of his insights into this problem. To contend that this is the central problem for Nietzsche as a philosopher does not do justice to the variety of topics and problems that Nietzsche addresses himself to, both within the corpus as a whole and within the works individually. The imagination of Nietzsche does not seem limited to one particular topic but it seems to burst with a richness found in a variety of themes and problems. The problem of reason is only one of these themes that dances with compelling movements between and through the seemingly inexhaustible variety of other subjects. It is not an alien theme, for its steps find a lively pattern and a tantalizing commonness with other topics. The present discussion of the problem develops only a few of these subjects in recognition of the fact that Nietzsche's philosophical concerns were far more extensive than the problem of reason.

To begin a discussion of the problem of the origin of reason, Nietzsche's aphorisms and short essays in the Götzen-Dämmerung oder Wie man mit dem Hammer Philosophirt are a good starting point because of their puthy character. In analyzing the title of this work it can be seen in a general way what Nietzsche attempted to do and how it illuminates the problem of reason. Götzen-Dämmerung is the title which is usually attached to this work and the remainder, oder Wie man mit dem Hammer Philosophirt, is usually omitted. In English this is translated as Twilight of the Idols which is only a translation of Götzen-Dämmerung.[1] In attempting to understand this title it should be recognized that part of the original title which is usually omitted, is of significance. Translated, this part of the title appears as How one Philosophizes with a Hammer. The significance of Nietzsche's philosophizing with a hammer becomes apparent after a look at the preface to this work.

---

1. The title appears in this way in both the Walter Kaufmann edition and the Oscar Levi edition. The Kaufmann translation of this work appears in a collection of works which is called The Portable Nietzsche, trans. and ed. by Walter Kaufmann (2nd ed.; New York: The Viking Press, 1954).

ESSAYS ON REASON, WILL, CREATIVITY, AND TIME

Studies in the Philosophy of Friedrich Nietzsche

Bernard Den Ouden
University of Hartford

UNIVERSITY
PRESS OF
AMERICA

University Press of America, Inc.

P.O. Box 19101, Washington, D.C. 20036

Printed in the United States of America

ISBN (Perfect): 0-8191-2450-8
ISBN (Cloth): 0-8191-2449-4

Library of Congress Catalog Card Number: 81-43491

TABLE OF CONTENTS

INTRODUCTION

The following three essays deal with a central theme in Nietzsche's philosophy, i.e., the nature and significance of human creativity. For Nietzsche there is but one good and that is to create. Understanding the "problem of reason," the reality of will, and the significance of the "eternal recurrence" is to discern the essential factors that contribute to or impinge upon the creative process.

The styles of the essays that follow differ. The first on "The Tyranny of Rationality" participates in the extreme hypothesis of Nietzsche's early authorship. In it Nietzsche's argument is pressed to its most exaggerated form. The plausibility of his perceptions is examined from what is taken to be his own intentionality. This essay also tests the image of Socrates and of Socratic rationality against primary and secondary sources.

The second essay, "An Interpretation of Nietzsche's Philosophy of the Will to Power," attempts to place Nietzsche's concepts of will and volitional activity within the tradition of German philosophy that extends from Kant through Fichte, Schelling, and Schopenhauer. Nietzsche's view of the will is interpreted as extending the problematics of this tradition and driving them to their logical conclusion. The relationship between the will and time is also examined. The will in its highest function for Nietzsche does not will blindly; it affirms itself and human life in the fertile moment of human creativity.

The eternal recurrence is directly examined in the third essay and is seen to be the synthesis and culmination of Nietzsche's thoughts concerning creativity.

The studies that follow should be contrasted by the reader with other views of Nietzsche's thought, especially Werner J. Dannhauser's Nietzsche's View of Socrates, Walter Kaufmann's Nietzsche, and Joan Stambaugh's excellent studies Nietzsche's Thought of Eternal Recurrence and Untersuchen Zum Problem Zeit Bei Nietzsche. The following essays are in no way intended to be exclusive interpretations of Nietzsche's philosophy but are studies that hopefully illuminate facets of his thought from assumptions and problematics that are interpretively appropriate to what the "philosopher psychologist and antichrist" was contributing to his culture and ours.

By philosophizing with a hammer, Nietzsche can strike at idols that are taken to be eternal. These idols, Nietzsche contends, will be proven to be false deities by the empty and hollow sound which they shall make as a result of being struck by the philosophical hammer.[2]

These idols are phenomena such as morality and reason, which are taken to be eternally valid for all mankind. They were not understood as phenomena which merely developed in the course of Western history, but as eternal gods that must not and cannot be questioned.

Nietzsche approaches the problem of reason in reference to the theme of cultural idols. Reason was a cultural idol which was deified by late Hellenism. The pivotal figure in bringing about this deification was Socrates. Nietzsche contends that Socrates did not promote the dominance of reason because he believed it to be in the eternal essence of reality. Socrates reacted to the dissolution and decay that was setting into Greek culture and in panic and reaction instituted reason. The instincts were playing the tyrant in Greek culture because the authority and restraint of the gods of Helles were being lost. Socrates saw that he must create a counter tyrant out of reason to check this dissolution and decay.

> When one finds it necessary to turn reason into tyrant, as Socrates did, the danger cannot be slight that something else will play the tyrant. Rationality was then hit upon as the savior; neither Socrates nor his "patients" had any choice about being rational: it was _de rigeur_, it was their last resort. The fanaticism with which all Greek reflection throws itself upon rationality betrays a desperate situation; there was danger, there was but one choice: either to perish or--to be _absurdly rational_. The moralism of the Greek philosophers from Plato on is pathologically conditioned; so is their esteem of dialectics. Reason-virtue-happiness, that means merely that one must imitate Socrates and counter the dark appetites with a permanent daylight--the daylight of reason. One must be clever, clear, bright at any price: any concession to the instincts, to the unconscious, leads downward.[3]

---

2. Friedrich Nietzsche, _Twilight of the Idols_, in _The Portable Nietzsche_, pp. 465-66.

3. _Ibid._, p. 478.

Nietzsche suggests that this movement to the absolute deification of reason was opposed to the genius of the pre-Socratic Helles. Nietzsche even goes so far as to say that Socrates was not Greek because of his ugliness:

> We know, we can still see for ourselves, how ugly he was. But ugliness, in itself an objection, is among the Greeks almost a refutation. Was Socrates a Greek at all? . . . A foreigner who knew about faces once passed through Athens and told Socrates to his face that he _was_ a _monstrum_--that he harbored in himself all the bad vices and appetites. And Socrates merely answered: "You know me, sir!"[4]

The significance of Socrates' ugliness as a refutation among the Greeks does not lie in the fact that Nietzsche through this bit of information has thoroughly proven that Socrates was not a Greek. The significance is rather that Nietzsche was so thoroughly convinced that Socrates was not Greek in his deification of reason that even his ugliness seemed to prove to Nietzsche his non-Greek nature. Nietzsche also finds Socrates' dialectics to be opposed to the genius of the Hellenic imagination. Dialectics were evidence of "bad manners" and "young men were warned against them."[5] Dialectics did not find a home in the nobility of the Greek imagination but resulted from Socrates' fascination with the combative instinct of the Greeks. The same instinct that attracted Socrates to the fencing arenas in Athens attracted and stimulated him to encourage the use of dialectics among his fellow Athenians.[6] Nietzsche continues to shade this picture of Socrates by means of comments concerning his death:

> Socrates _wanted_ to die: not Athens, but he himself chose the hemlock; he forced Athens to sentence him. "Socrates is no physician," he said softly to himself; "here death alone is the physician. Socrates himself has merely been sick a long time."[7]

---

4. _Ibid._, pp. 474-75.

5. _Ibid._, p. 475.

6. Plato, _Plato, Laches, Protagoras, Meno, Euthydemus_, (272E), E. Capps, T.E. Page, and W.H.D. Rouse, ed., trans. by W.R.M. Lamb (9 vols.: London: William Heinemann, 1914-1926. New York: G.P. Putnam's Sons, 1914-1926), IV, pp. 380-381. In the _Euthydemus_ it is suggested that Socrates frequented the circles of the fencing masters.

7. Friedrich Nietzsche, _Twilight of the Idols_, p. 479.

Socrates as a doctor saw himself as a failure. What could have provoked this thought? Why did Socrates wish to die? In healing Greek culture from its illness and decay, Socrates had administered reason as a cure. But what were the effects of reason? Reason seemed at a superficial level to give the trembling culture of Greece a bit of equilibrium; however, as can be seen in an analysis of other of Nietzsche's works, reason killed the culture it supposedly was to cure. In turning to The Birth of Tragedy, Nietzsche describes clearly just how reason brought about the death of the Greek imagination and creativity, and thereby Greek culture.

There are many themes at work in The Birth of Tragedy. The effect of the dominance of reason is only one of the themes. Related to the theme of reason are many other topics, only one of them shall be mentioned. This is a problem that looms in the background and is Nietzsche's concern for the lack of genuine culture in Germany. One of the reasons for this is that the Germans who could possibly create a culture are hopelessly restrained. They are restrained because they allow intellectual and cultural idols to choke the possibility for growth. A specific form of being choked and thus being unable to grow intellectually results from the dominance of reason. In freeing itself from the dominance of reason, German culture can learn from Greek culture the course of its imaginative genius and also how this genius can be, and was in fact, lost.[8]

In The Birth of Tragedy the origin and effect of reason are discussed in the context of Greek tragedy. In the early sections of this essay Nietzsche describes how the Hellenic genius originated and developed. The essence of the Hellenic genius, according to Nietzsche, was the free interplay of the Apollonian and the Dionysian. The Apollonian,taking its name from the god Apollo, represents one of two realities, or "worlds of art." The Apollonian represents form, individuation, and restraint. This is the god of the plastic arts, the deity of clarity and light. It creates a beautiful illusion which takes the form of an image or a dream. Its music is architectonic and its thought is pure, rational contemplation of images and ideals. It is the sublime taming of reality into intelligibility and form.

---

8. Friedrich Nietzsche, The Birth of Tragedy, in The Birth of Tragedy and the Case of Wagner, trans. and ed. by Walter Kaufmann (New York: Vintage Books of Random House, 1967), p. 31.

For Apollo wants to grant repose to individual beings precisely by drawing boundaries between them and by again and again calling these to mind as the most sacred laws of the world, with his demands for self-knowledge and measure.[9]

The Apollonian represents the tendency in Greek culture to limit and to confine the Hellenic will or spirit. This limitation was the limitation of form, measure, and individuation. It was the capturing and confining of the boundless.

The partner in play for the Apollonian is the Dionysian. The Dionysian originates in the boundless and the chaotic. It is unformed and not individuated. It does not know restraint and peace unless it is held in tension by the Apollonian. In its primitive form, that is, without the restraint of Apollonian subjugation, the Dionysian is very similar to the ecstasy of a wild and frenzied dance in which a harmony is felt that is much deeper than the level of conscious reflection. In this ecstasy a primal unity and harmony dominates all that is and the dancer loses his or her individuality and consciousness. He or she is the primal unity. They are the chaos and pain that seeks form in appearance. The dancer is thus in tune with the essence and origin of reality. This essence or ground of reality is without form and individuation. It is the flow of the totality behind all that is.[10] When the individual participates in this ground they seem to be possessed or intoxicated. The individual is possessed and intoxicated by the "all." Nietzsche, in comparing the Dionysian and the Apollonian, contends that the Apollonian is best expressed in the rigid and clear lines of the plastic arts. The Dionysian is best conveyed in music because of music's ability to create the formless and to follow the pain and ecstasy of the will and the emotions. The Dionysian could also be described as the unstructured unconscious which is chaotic and without form. When given form and symbolization the Dionysian appears in a dream. It has been individuated and shaped but its origin was still the chaotic unconscious. The Apollonian form and symbolization gives the Dionysian intelligibility and thus shapes the chaotic into symbols and images.

---

9. Ibid., p. 72.

10. Ibid., pp. 99-100.

The relationship between the Apollonian and the Dionysian, as Nietzsche imaginatively describes it, is similar to the relationship between sexual partners: "the continuous development of art is bound up with the Apollonian and Dionysian duality--just as procreation depends on the duality of the sexes, involving perpetual strife with only periodically intervening reconciliations."[11] The rational Apollonian pursues and subdues the mysterious and unintelligible Dionysian until the Dionysian is brought to rest in form and intelligibility. It is in this process that Nietzsche finds the genius of Greek creativity. The Greek spirit flashes with blinding creativity as long as the Apollonian and Dionysian are allowed to function freely. When the Apollonian is lost, all that remains is chaos and unintelligibility. When the Dionysian is lost the Apollonian becomes pure abstract form and does not issue from the source of reality. The Dionysian and the Apollonian are of equal importance because they are helpless without each other. In The Birth of Tragedy Nietzsche does not give one a more important role than the other; it is through strife and reconciliation that creativity arises. This requires both the Apollonian and the Dionysian.

> In The Birth of Tragedy, Nietzsche did not extol one at the expense of the other; but if he favors one of the two gods, it is Apollo. His thesis is that it took both to make possible the birth of tragedy, and he emphasizes the Dionysian only because he feels that the Apollonian genius of the Greeks cannot be fully understood apart from it.[12]

This balance between the Dionysian and the Apollonian Nietzsche finds to operate freely in early Hellenism and especially in Greek tragedy. Nietzsche cites Aeschylus and Sophocles as examples of dramatists who promoted the free play of the Dionysian and the Apollonian. In their drama the chorus was the foremost Dionysian element:

> . . . we must understand Greek tragedy as the Dionysian chorus which ever anew discharges itself in an Apollonian world of images . . .

---

11. Ibid., p. 33.

12. Walter Kaufmann, Nietzsche, Philosopher, Psychologist, Antichrist (2nd ed.; Cleveland and New York: The World Publishing Co., 1950), p. 108.

> _Dionysus_, the real stage hero and center of the vision, was, according both to this insight and to the tradition, not actually present at first, in the very oldest period of tragedy; he was merely imagined as present, which means that originally tragedy was only "chorus" and not yet "drama." Later the attempt was made to show the god as real and to represent the visionary figure together with its transfiguring frame as something visible for every eye--and thus "drama" in the narrower sense began. Now the dithrambic chorus was assigned the task of exciting the mood of the listeners to such a Dionysian degree that, when the tragic hero appeared on the stage, they did not see the awkwardly masked human being but rather a visionary figure, born as it were from their own rapture.[13]

The Dionysian element was recognized and experienced in a variety of ways in the early form of Greek tragedy. The chorus, as we have seen, was the center for the Dionysian element in the drama. The individual who attended the drama who would ordinarily be called a spectator was in fact not a spectator. He or she felt himself to be part of the chorus or lost personal consciousness in the totality of the artistic production. The participant did not remain essentially apart and removed from the artistic activity; but in a Dionysian manner, lost his or her individuality. The participant, however, did not allow the Dionysian to exclude personal apprehension of the Apollonian. The dialogue at the surface appeared to be "simple, transparent, and beautiful."[14] Nietzsche, like the participant, does not turn his back on the precision and lucidity of the language of Sophocles' heroes. However, he does emphasize the dark background of mystery against which the bright images of the Apollonian are projected. Thus, the Apollonian does not exclude the Dionysian,or vice versa; that is, the brightness and lucidity do not exclude the mystery but their realities are enhanced by the mutuality of their play. To see how this phenomenon is operative,a close look at the tragic hero himself can complement what has been discussed concerning the chorus and the participant, the spectator who is not a spectator but a participant.

As Nietzsche paints the picture, the tragic hero is Dionysus:

---

13. Friedrich Nietzsche, _The Birth of Tragedy_, pp. 64-66.

14. _Ibid_., p. 67.

The tradition is undisputed that Greek tragedy in its earliest form had for its sole theme the sufferings of Dionysus and that for a long time the only stage hero was Dionysus himself. But it may be claimed with equal confidence that until Euripides, Dionysus never ceased to be the tragic hero; that all the celebrated figures of the Greek stage--Prometheus, Oedipus, etc.--are mere masks of this original hero, Dionysus . . . the Greeks simply could not suffer individuals on the tragic stage. In fact, this is what they seem to have felt; and the Platonic distinction and evaluation of the "idea" and the "idol," the mere image, is very deeply rooted in the Hellenic character.

Using Plato's terms we should have to speak of the tragic figures of the Hellenic stage somewhat as follows: the one truly real Dionysus appears in a variety of forms, in the mask of a fighting hero, and entangled as it were, in the net of the individual will. The god who appears talks and acts so as to resemble an erring, striving, suffering individual. That he appears at all with such epic precision and clarity is the work of the dream-interpreter, Apollo, who through this symbolic appearance interprets to the chorus its Dionysian state. In truth, however, the hero is the suffering Dionysus of the Mysteries, the god experiencing in himself the agonies of individuation, of whom wonderful myths tell that as a boy he was torn to pieces by the Titans and now is worshipped in this state as Zagreus.[15]

It is not insignificant that the struggle of the tragic hero is described as the agony of individuation. Individuation is none other than the fusion of the Apollonian with the Dionysian. In this fusion the Dionysian element feels the pain and pressure of being bounded in and cramped into individuality. The Apollonian restrains and restricts, but in doing so brings the captured Dionysian into the light of intelligibility.

The early form of Greek tragedy allowed for the free play of the Dionysian and Apollonian. However, as Nietzsche contends, this is not the case for late Hellenism. With the advent of Euripides a radical change occurred in Greek drama. First of all, Euripides brought spectators back into the audience. The spectator was now truly a spectator and was no longer a participant, as was true for the earlier form of Greek drama. The spectator was essentially apart from the artistic activity because he or she was encouraged to pass judgment on the drama.

---

15. Ibid., p. 73.

As Nietzsche suggests there were two spectators that were of particular significance to Euripides: "Of these two spectators, one is Euripides, himself, Euripides as thinker, not as poet."[16] Euripides as a thinker found something mysterious and unintelligible behind every aspect of the older tragedy. This he could not tolerate. He felt the uncertainty and the lack of clarity must be abolished. All the ethical problems that were involved in this drama were dubious. There were no clear answers. Ambiguity seemed to be the background for all the scenes; moral and intellectual chaos seemed ready to break through at any moment.

Euripides shared this viewpoint with a second spectator. This spectator was none other than Socrates. Socrates commanded Euripides' respect and was taken by Euripides to be a competent judge of the value of drama. Socrates was antagonistic to the older form of Greek tragedy. He warned his acquaintances against attending the theatre: "Socrates, as an opponent of tragic art, refrained from attending tragedies and appeared among the spectators only when a new play of Euripides was to be performed."[17] Nietzsche offers more significant evidence for the allegiance of Socrates and Euripides against the darkness and mystery of the early Greek drama. According to Nietzsche, the contemporaries of Socrates and Euripides thought that Socrates would help Euripides write his plays. This may or may not have been rumor, but the point seems apparent. Euripides and Socrates found a great deal of commonality.[18] Socrates and Euripides were concerned with saving the culture of Greece. They wanted to save it from decay and immorality. They took the root and source of this decay to be the darkness and unintelligibility that was found in facets of their culture and, as a result, in drama. This was none other than the Dionysian, the mysterious, and the chaotic which danced in unintelligibility behind all reality. The Dionysian, as Euripides and Socrates saw it, must be driven from Greek soil. It was a constant source of ambiguity and uncertainty in intellectual pursuits and in morality.

---

16. Ibid., p. 80.

17. Ibid., p. 87.

18. Walter Kaufmann, Tragedy and Philosophy (Garden City, New York: Doubleday and Company, Inc., 1968), p. 244. Here Kaufmann contends that Euripides influenced Socrates. The relationship between these two men, at any rate, seems significantly close.

> Is the Dionysian entitled to exist at all? Should it not be forcibly uprooted from Hellenic soil? Certainly, the poet tells us. . . Dionysus had already been scared from the tragic stage, by a demonic power speaking through Euripides. Even Euripides was, in a sense, only a mask: The deity that spoke through him was neither Dionysus nor Apollo, but an altogether newborn demon, Socrates.
>
> This is the new opposition: the Dionysian and the Socratic--and the art of Greek tragedy was wrecked on this. Though Euripides may seek to comfort us by his recantation, he does not succeed: the most magnificent temple lies in ruins. What does the lamentation of the destroyer profit us, or his confession that it was the most beautiful of all temples? And even if Euripides has been punished by being changed into a dragon by the art critics of all ages--who could be content with so miserable a compensation?[19]

As can be seen from the above statement, Nietzsche suggests that Euripides realized the consequences of his activities. Nietzsche suggests the same for Socrates, as we have seen previously in discussing the statements of Nietzsche concerning Socrates' death. However, Nietzsche suggests, their regret had no effect because the crime had been committed. In cutting a bit deeper we can see the actual atrocity that Socrates and Euripides brought about and which in the end they realized and regretted.

The Socratic tendency, as it becomes apparent in the work of Euripides, finds its essence in cool and abstract thoughts. The spectator at the drama of Euripides was entertained with paradoxes and the quirks of thought that reason can expose. Reason and intelligibility had now become virtues. All that would hope to pass for truth must now pass before the clear light of reason and intelligibility. This meant that the Euripidean hero would spend a greater part of his time reviewing his actions

---

19. Friedrich Nietzsche, The Birth of Tragedy, pp. 81-82.

in a conscious and extremely rational fashion.[20] There was no toleration in this framework for the poet who created unconsciously. As Nietzsche contends, Socrates and Euripides made an absolute out of conscious knowledge:

> Euripides undertook to show to the world the reverse of the "unintelligent" poet; his aesthetic principle that "to be beautiful everything must be conscious" is, as I have said, the parallel to the Socratic, "to be good everything must be conscious."[21]

Thus, the poet who created when he was bereft of his understanding was assigned to a role of insignificance.

With the advent of Socrates and Euripides, rationality and conscious thought became the critics of creativity and truth. All that was a product of the imagination was trimmed and possibly leveled before the precise blade of rationality. The gateway to the mysterious dark and the freely imaginative was firmly closed. A sign of severe warning was placed at this gate. This sign read: Behind this gate lies the essence of destruction and chaos. Unleash this darkness and we will all tumble into ruin. As a result of this warning the unconscious, mysterious, and non-rational aspects of man's intellect were pushed further and further into obscurity. The imagination was torn from this mysterious root of reality and restricted to the imagining of the abstract. Reason became the only aspect of the intellect that commanded respectability. All other aspects of the intellect were exiled into obscurity. It is essentially the beginning of this dominance of reason that Nietzsche calls to our attention in the advent

---

20. Bruno Snell, The Discovery of the Mind, The Greek Origins of European Thought, trans. by T.G. Rosenmeyer (2nd ed.; New York and Evanston: Harper & Ros, 1960), pp. 124-125. Bruno Snell has this to say about Euripides' Medea and Nietzsche:

> "Euripides Medea is wholly written around the monologue in which Medea makes up her mind to murder her children . . . The perspective of Nietzsche was clearer than that of Aristophanes or Schlegel. The fond ideals of religious tradition are unmasked and demolished so that a truer justice may be discovered, and its claim staked out. And who would fail to be impressed with the justice of Medea's case?"

21. Friedrich Nietzsche, The Birth of Tragedy, p. 86.

of Socrates and Euripides. It is in this dominance that Nietzsche sees the death of the truly creative and artistic. The death is caused by the restriction of the imagination to that which is rational.

It would seem from various scholars who have dealt with Nietzsche and the problem of reason that their viewpoints have been focused toward the issue of whether or not Nietzsche admired or despised Socrates. The majority of scholars seem to have emphasized Nietzsche's criticism of Socrates and, in view of this criticism, they have concluded that Nietzsche took Socrates to be a villain.[22] Walter Kaufmann contributes to this discussion and attempts to demonstrate the opposite, that is, he attempts to show how much Nietzsche admired Socrates.[23] This issue of whether or not Nietzsche liked or disliked, admired or despised, loved or hated Socrates seems ironically to miss the importance of Nietzsche's work concerning Socrates and reason. Nietzsche acutely understood the advent of Socrates as a shift in the Western intellect and consciousness. This shift, as Nietzsche saw it, had a tremendous effect; it was not solely the work of Socrates. In Socrates the most significant expression of this shift can be found. Socrates gathered together the tendencies toward rationalism which he found among the sophists and other facets of Greek culture. These tendencies he focused into one absolute which is called rational thought. It cannot be denied that Nietzsche felt intensely about Socrates. "Socrates, to confess it frankly, is so close to me that almost always I struggle against him."[24] However, this intensity was not grounded in a superficial love or hate. This intensity was based on Nietzsche's acute intuition into the magnitude and effect that the idol of Socrates, with his cult of rationalism, would and did

---

22. Crane Brinton, Nietzsche (Cambridge: Harvard University Press, 1941), p. 83. Brinton is an example of one of these scholars.

23. Walter Kaufmann, Nietzsche, pp. 334-352.

24. Friedrich Nietzsche, Nietzsche's Werke (15 vols.; Leipzig: C.G. Naumann, 1900-1906), X, p. 217. Translation mine.

have on the Western intellect and imagination.[25]

In looking to another work of Nietzsche's, that is Schopenhauer, as Educator, another facet of Nietzsche's understanding of the problem of reason can be examined. In Schopenhauer, as Educator Nietzsche considers the significance of the life style of the philosopher. In this essay Nietzsche uses Schopenhauer as an example of a philosopher whose life style coresponds directly with his thought. As Walter Kaufmann points out, this example is merely a screen for Nietzsche's self-projections. In this essay Nietzsche describes what he is and what he hopes to be.

> Admittedly, this is not a literally correct historical portrait of Schopenhauer but only a device by which Nietzsche hopes to envisage his own true self--not deep inside, but "immeasurably high above" his present ego.[26]

The concern over the life style of the philosopher breaks into two foci. The first of these foci is that philosophy has allowed itself only to be concerned with reason and, in the case of the century preceding Nietzsche, only with pure reason. This has limited philosophizing concerning man to only one facet of man's intellect. Nietzsche suggests that German philosophers would profit far more from taking Schopenhauer as a model (actually Nietzsche as a model) than from concerning themselves with the nature and content of pure reason.[27] Philosophizing concerning reason remains in the realm of the abstract; using Schopenhauer as a model finds reality in existence.

---

25. Walter Kaufmann, Nietzsche, pp. 334-352. Kaufmann describes Nietzsche's attitude toward Socrates as "ambiguous" and constructs "a systematic inquiry...concerning Nietzsche's admiration for Socrates." (pp. 334-335). Kaufmann gathers together the fragments that are evidence for the fact that Nietzsche took Socrates extremely seriously and concludes:

> "As a dialectical thinker, Nietzsche affirms as necessary and admires even what must be overcome. His admiration does not arrest his thinking, and his critique does not detract from his admiration. In his own historical situation, Socrates acted as wisely and courageously as was then possible; but in the same passage Nietzsche claims that Socrates was a pessimist who "suffered life" as a disease." (p. 343).

26. Walter Kaufmann, Nietzsche, p. 136.

27. Friedrich Nietzsche, Schopenhauer als Erzieher, in Nietzsche's Werke (Leipzig: C.G. Naumann, 1905), I, pp. 387-392.

The second of these foci is the desire and actualization of fearlessness in the pursuit of truth. Nietzsche sees very little of this in contemporaries. What he does find are University professors who claim to be, or are falsely regarded as, philosophers. Their philosophy is adjusted to their position. Their concern is not with truth but with keeping their positions and possibly advancing in the hierarchy. Their life is as superficial as their philosophies. Among these men Nietzsche finds no relentless desire for truth. These men do not seem to possess the courage that Nietzsche calls for in his writings and demonstrates in his life. A clear example of this demonstration was Nietzsche publishing The Birth of Tragedy. This book flew in the face of contemporary research both in philosophy and philology: "The Birth of Tragedy presented a view of the Greeks so alien to the spirit of the time and to the ideals of its scholarship that it blighted Nietzsche's entire academic career."[28]

This fearlessness Nietzsche exhibited in yet another way. Nietzsche has often been accused of inconsistent thinking. This arises from his shift of position on various problems. This shift can be found when we look at different works within the Nietzsche corpus. To call it inconsistency is to meet this phenomenon at a superficial level. Nietzsche in his philosophizing possessed the courage to ride out the ambiguities of his own position. If this meant undercutting what he had contended previously, Nietzsche undercut with vigorous haste. Nietzsche did not need the security of a consistent philosophical position. This can be seen in the propensity to destroy the traditional philosophical idols which were crutches for the Western intellect. Nietzsche desires a free flowing and fearless imagination that never rests but continuously seeks new forms and understanding.

The phenomenon of pure reason is an acute example of the purely abstract and Apollonia. Pure reason finds its essence in being, absolute form, and abstraction. It is not informed by the mysterious, dark, or chaotic. It is pure and intelligible. As a result, the philosopher who makes pure reason his central concern is completely cut off from the creative interplay of the Dionysian and the Apollonia. He or she has lost the Dionysian or has allowed the Apollonian to exile the Dionysian. Here there is no pssibility of thought integrating into the life of

---

28. Marianne Cowan, "Introduction" in Friedrich Nietzsche's Philosophy in the Tragic Age of the Greeks, trans. by Marianne Cowan (Chicago: Henry Regnery Company, 1962), p. 4.

the individual unless the individual wants to lose the many facets of his intellect and existence for the sake of cool and abstract thoughts.[29]

The second of these foci, that is, fearlessness in the desire and actualization of truth, is treated as a cultural idol that Nietzsche fearlessly undercuts. Rational philosophy has traditionally refused to undercut rationality. Reason has been taken to be in the nature of reality eternal and unquestionable. Nietzsche hits this eternal idol head on and waits to see how it survives the crash. It would seem that rationality has survived the scrutiny to which Nietzsche subjected it. However, as can be seen, both rationality and the Greeks have been subjected to severe evaluations since the blinding and illuminating insights of Nietzsche first appeared. In the following chapters some of the insights concerning Socrates and the origin of reason that have evolved since the time of Nietzsche shall be evaluated.

In briefly looking at attitudes towards the Greeks it is clear that Nietzsche is not alone in his contention. In _Philosophy in the Tragic Age of the Greeks_, as well as the other of Nietzsche's works that we have considered, we see Nietzsche assign a definite superiority to pre-Socratic Greece. This is the Golden Age of Greece. This is the time when the Greek spirit flashed in dazzling creativity. In this age philosophy was not lost in abstract thought. In fact, abstract thought is labeled by Nietzsche as "un-Greek,"[30] and as a result of a later influence. This later influence was none other than the development of rationalism. This development was a symptom of decline, decay, and disintegration.

> So much depends on the development of Greek culture because our entire occidental world has received its initial stimuli from it. An adverse fate decreed that the late and decadent forms of Hellenism should exert the greatest historical influence. On their

---

29. The word cool in this context signifies passionless detachment which attempts to force thought into purity. "Cool" also conveys the separation of thought from the "hot" emotions.

30. Friedrich Nietzsche, _Philosophy in the Tragic Age of the Greeks_, p. 69.

account, earlier Hellenism has always been misjudged.[31]

Philosophers in this century have also emphasized the validity of this contrast. A prime example of this is Heidegger who assigns more significance to pre-Socratic Greece than any other period in Western thought.[32] Thus the pre-Socratics have been subjected to more consideration than the gods of philosophy--Socrates and Plato. In addition to this, if Socrates and Plato are considered, a great deal more is made of their seemingly irrational tendencies.[33]

In order to bind together the insights that have been discovered with the aid of Nietzsche, the core of the present essay can be elucidated. The argument being presented is that rationalism if elevated to a position of tyranny can restrain and restrict the imagination. Reason, which is merely one facet of the intellect and imagination, attempts to dominate other capacities.

---

31. Friedrich Nietzsche, Nietzsche's Werke, Vol. X, p. 219. Translation mine.

> "Er hängst soviel von der Entwicklung der griechischen Cultur ab, da unsre ganse abändlandische Welt daher ihre Antriebe becommen hat: das Verhängniss Wollte, dass das jüngere und entartete Griechenthum am meisten historische Kraft gezeight hat. Darüber ist das ältere Griechenthum immer falsche beurtheilt worden."

32. Martin Heidegger, An Introduction to Metaphysics, trans. by Ralph Manheim (2nd ed.; Garden City, New York: Doubleday & Company, Inc., 1961), passim, chap. 3.

33. We will discuss an example of this in the next chapter especially in view of E.R. Dodds' The Greeks and the Irrational (Berkeley and Los Angeles: University of California Press, 1966) and Josef Pieper's Enthusiasm and Divine Madness in the Platonic Dialogue Phaedrus, translated by Richard and Clara Winston (New York: Harcourt, Brace, and World, Inc., 1964) in which both Socrates and Plato are viewed as recognizing the significance of the irrational.

This domination only allows the imagination to depict abstract symbols and forms. Thus, that which proceeds from the imagination in the form of expression is restricted to the rational. The imagination, which is far broader than reason, is restricted to reason. This restriction to reason cuts the intellect off from the realm of the dark, mysterious, and the chaotic. This is the life-giving womb of of creative reality. It is the abyss of nothingness out of which being, reality and meaning proceed.[34] For Nietzsche this is the realm of the unconscious. This is the realm that can only be known through glimpses and fragments, that is, only through symbols and forms that slip through to consciousness and await understanding. In this framework the essence of creativity is taken to be the free play of the realm of the mysterious with the form-giving reality of symbolization. This has been seen previously in Nietzsche's description of the Apollonian and the Dionysian. In Nietzsche's framework, clarity, intelligibility, and form do not exclude the mysterious, but play with it and seduce it into images and symbols. Thus the symbols and images are always in contact with the dark and mysterious and are not isolated to the realm of the abstract.

To test the validity of the interpretation that has been developed with the aid of Nietzsche's insights, the position that Plato and Socrates assumed against the tragic poet shall be analyzed. This position will be examined to see if it reflects the tyranny of reason. This course will be assumed as a means of testing the contention at hand, which is that with the philosophies of Plato and Socrates reason rose to a position of tyranny.

---

34. This realm is often referred to in Nietzsche's The Birth of Tragedy:

> ". . . his oneness with the innermost ground of the world (p. 38) . . . that mysterious ground of our being (p. 44) . . . while by the triumphant cry of Dionysus the spell of individuation is broken, and the way lies open to the Mothers of Being, to the innermost heart of things." (pp. 99-100).

CHAPTER II

PLATO, SOCRATES, AND THE TRAGIC POET

"In the creative state a man is taken out of himself. He lets down as it were a bucket into his subconscious, and draws up something which is normally beyond his reach."

E. M. Forster

To leave the insights of Nietzsche at the level of mere exposition and clarification would be highly unsatisfactory. Both the manner in which Nietzsche presents his insights concerning the origin of reason and their radical import demand further discussion. Pushing forward would seem to necessitate a form of verification, that is, testing the insights to see if they illuminate the problem with which they are concerned. There is, however, a preliminary matter that requires consideration because it directly involves the methodology which will be assumed. This arises out of Nietzsche's "Attempt at a Self Criticism," which appears as a preface to the "new edition" of The Birth of Tragedy which appeared in 1886.[35] In this brief statement Nietzsche refers to The Birth of Tragedy as "questionable" and "audacious." He patently admits that the style and manner in which the book was written reflect the cavalier tendency of his youth, but he does not compromise the thrust of his original statement. However, the fact that Nietzsche regards his own book as cavalier, audacious, and questionable seems further to demand that we expose his insights to some evaluation. The most crucial phenomenon to which these criticisms of Nietzsche refer is the blatant lack of documentation in The Birth of Tragedy.[36] Nietzsche weaves his representation of the Greeks and the origin of reason with little reference to specific sources in the Greek literature. This presents an acute problem for the evaluation of these insights. In order to circumvent this problem, Nietzsche's insights will be tested against the specific literature which appeared in the era with which he was concerned.

To begin this testing, the posture that Plato assumes against poetry in the Republic is significant. The focal point for this position appears in Part VI of Book X.[37] Poetry and the poet are of special importance because, Nietzsche contends, the tragic poet and the dark mysterious aspect of his work were the central targets in the reaction of reason. In the Republic the validity of this contention can be tested.

---

35. The Birth of Tragedy originally appeared in 1872.

36. This is also the case for Twilight of the Idols and Philosophy in the Tragic Age of the Greeks.

37. Plato, The Republic of Plato, trans. with Introduction and Notes by Francis M. Cornford (New York and London: Oxford University Press, 1945), pp. 321-40.

In discussing the type of "commonwealth" that would bring about the best situation for mankind, Socrates and the men with which he is engaging in a dialogue come to the conclusion that dramatic poetry should be excluded.

> Indeed, I continue, our commonwealth has many features which make me think it was based on very sound principles, especially our rule not on any account to admit the poetry of dramatic representation. Now that we have distinguished the several parts of the soul, it seems to me clearer than ever that such poetry must be firmly excluded....poetry of that sort seems to be injurious to minds that do not possess the antidote in a knowledge of its real nature.[38]

Thus, inherent in the nature of poetry there existed a danger, a disease which could be contacted by exposure of the intellect to poetry. This disease could be cured by the proper administration of an antidote. This antidote took the form of knowledge of poetry's "real nature."

To begin his analysis of the nature of poetry, Plato had Socrates recapitulate the theory of the ideal forms.[39] In this discussion Socrates assumes what he designates as usual procedure and refers to a single form "for every set of things which we call by the same name."[40] He then proceeds to exemplify this by referring to a single form for tables and a single form for beds. There are any number of tables and beds but only one form for beds and tables respectively. The particular bed that Socrates slept on depended for its reality on the degree to which this particular bed represented or resembled the ideal form for beds. The craftsmen in his construction of Socrates' bed had attempted to represent the ideal form of beds. The craftsman in his representation only at best constructed a phenomenon that was once removed from reality, that is, the particular bed could only be patterned after reality and thus was not one with reality. As Socrates drives the inquiry further he seeks to delineate the nature of the work of the artist.

---

38. Ibid., p. 324.

39. Ibid., p. 325.

40. Ibid.

The artist, in painting a picture of a bed, is representing a particular bed. He is mirroring the appearance of this bed but is not in actuality reproducing all the qualities of the bed he is painting: for example, he is not producing a bed on which he can sleep. The artist represents a representation. The first bed which was constructed by the carpenter was a representation of the ideal bed. The artist's work is thus a representation of the carpenter's representation. The carpenter's work was described as once removed from reality and thus it would seem that the work of the artist would be twice removed from reality.[41] The thrust of Socrates' discussion, however, was not intended as an explication of the nature of beds, tables, or any particular object. The thrust was also not directed to the work of carpenters or of painters. In fact, the real object for the discussion was the tragic poet. The discussion of beds, tables, carpenters, and painters was only a technique to reach Socrates' understanding of the tragic poet. "The tragic poet, too, is an artist who represents things; so this will apply to him."[42] The poet like the artist only represented appearances and thus his work at best had a slight resemblance of reality. The tragic poet like the artist could only represent human activity. He could not reproduce human activity as it was but only as it appeared. "The art of representation, then, is a long way from reality."[43] The work of the poet, as of the artist, is even inferior to the work of the carpenter. It is at best a semblance of reality and it is likely to confuse the individual who is exposed to it. Furthermore, if it is merely a semblance, its representation is likely to be illusory.

On account of the illusory nature of his work, the poet is seen to be a threat to the society that Plato proposed. This threat is so significant that the philosopher must take it upon himself to destroy the power of the threat and cure the minds of the people who are already affected. This cure requires an antidote which is none other than a knowledge of the nature of poetry. But to what type of knowledge is Plato referring? Clearly it is rational knowledge that brings the mind to absolute clarity and banishes the illusory mystery of the poetic influence. It would

---

41. Ibid., p. 327.

42. Ibid.

43. Ibid., p. 328.

seem from what Plato has stated, that Nietzsche's description of Socrates as a cultural physician is accurate. The cure Socrates administered was also decidedly rational. In addition to this, it is patently obvious that the cure, reason, was directed to fight off the influence of the tragic poet. But why is the tragic poet so threatening to Socrates and Plato? Or what does the antagonism of Plato and Socrates reflect concerning the influence of the poets? Clearly their influence was substantial. The history of Greek culture was rehearsed and recapitulated in the work of the poet. The mythologies and epics were alluded to and given new expression in each dramatic presentation.[44] The individual was thus reunited with his cultural heritage through the work of the poet.

It was this influence that Plato and Socrates sought to squelch. It was an influence that was penetrated with mystery and ambiguity. In fact, in questioning the poets, Socrates found that they could not give a rational account of what they were saying or projecting:

> For after the statesmen, I approached the poets, the composers of tragedies and the composers of dithyrams, and all the rest as well; there I expected to find myself caught in the act as more ignorant than they were. So I took up their poems, those which I thought they had taken most pains to perfect, and questioned them as to what they meant, and I hoped to learn something from them at the same time. Well, gentlemen, I am ashamed to tell you the truth; but I must. Almost all the bystanders with hardly an exception, one might say, had something better to say than the composers had about their own compositions. I discovered, then, very soon about the poets that no wisdom enabled them to compose as they did, but natural genius and inspiration; like the diviners and those who chant oracles, who say many fine things but do not understand anything of what they say. The poets appeared to me to be in much the same case; and at the same time I perceived that

---

44. Bruno Snell, The Discovery of the Mind, p. 122. Snell describes the relationship between Greek mythology and Greek tragedy in this way: "To be sure, attic drama never turned profane, for almost without exception its subject matter continued to be myth."

> because of their poetry they believed they were the wisest of mankind in other things as well, which they were not. So I left them also, believing that I had the same superiority over them as I have over the statesmen.[45]

The poet could not give Socrates evidence that he had a rational justification for what he had written in his poetry. He also could not rationally understand what he had written in his own works. There was, as a result, a deep level of unintelligibility in the work of the poet. It was penetrated with mystery, a mystery that the poet himself could not understand or force into rational clarity even if he had given the mystery form in his poetic language.

In yet another way Socrates poses the case for the exclusion of the poet from the commonwealth. The poet, through the means of his dramatic productions, exaggerates human feelings and emotions. This exaggeration creates an illusion that appeals to the spectator. In previous discussions in the Republic, Socrates had concluded that the soul was divided into three parts. The lowest and most degraded of these parts was the "lower part, the emotions." It was to this aspect of the soul that the poet appealed. There was, however, according to Socrates, a cure for this illusory effect that influenced the emotions. "But satisfactory means have been found for dispelling these illusions. . . And this can only be the work of the calculating or reasoning element of the soul."[46] The higher part of the soul thus clarified and destroyed the base illusions that drama had effected. These illusions would inevitably contradict what the rational part of the soul found to be the case and thus the higher part of the soul would eliminate the fantasies which had captured the emotions.

Plato continues to shade his conception of poetry's effect by describing its influence on character. "Dramatic poetry has a most formidable power of corrupting even men of high character with few exceptions."[47] This results from the spectator's identification with the suffering and lamenting of the stage hero. The spectator finds it to be extremely pleasurable to lose himself in

---

45. Plato, The Apology, in Great Dialogues of Plato, ed. by Eric H. Warmington and Philip G. Rouse with trans. by W.H.D. Rouse (New York: The New American Library, 1956), p. 428.

46. Plato, The Republic of Plato, p. 334.

47. Ibid., p. 337.

the tirades and anguish of the hero. In actual life the spectator would be greatly embarrassed if he or any of acquaintances behaved in that way. However, the feelings that were presented on the stage were not his own and as a result it was very enjoyable to float with their crests and falls. This experience, according to Plato, would definitely have an adverse effect on character. "It waters the growth of passion which should be allowed to wither away and sets them up in control, although the goodness and happiness of our lives depends on their being held in subjection."[48] Dramatic poetry, according to Plato, cultivates the activity of the emotions. This, he contends, is highly undesirable because living the "good and virtuous life" demands that the emotions be suppressed and subjugated.[49]

In the Gorgias we find a slightly different variation of essentially the same criticism. The situation or context for this dialogue was the encounter of Socrates with the famous rhetorician Gorgias. Socrates questioned Gorgias concerning the content and purpose of his discipline. In the course of the discussion Socrates had forced Gorgias to admit that the only accomplishment attained by a rhetorician is that of giving his audience pleasure. In establishing this point Socrates compared the orators and rhetoricians to the poets.

---

48. Ibid., pp. 338-39.

49. Walter Kaufmann, Tragedy and Philosophy, p. 24. Kaufmann makes this comment concerning Plato's program in the Republic:

> "There is something inhumane about a program designed to let the passions wither away, an education designed to train each man and woman for one role, and a systematic attempt to keep from them poetry that might enlarge their sympathies and make them aware of their own manifold potentialities. In his concern for virtue and happiness--it is really serenity rather than happiness--Plato becomes a prophet of austerity and puritanism."

> Socrates: Then what of the purpose that has inspired our stately and wonderful tragic poetry? Are her endeavour and purpose to your mind, merely for the gratification of the spectators, or does she strive hard, if there be anything pleasant and gratifying but bad for them, to leave that unsaid, and if there be anything unpleasant, but beneficial, both speak and sing that, whether they enjoy it or not? To which of these two aims, think you, is tragic poetry devoted? Callicles: It is quite obvious, in her case, Socrates, that she is bent rather upon pleasure and the gratification of the spectators.
>
> . . . .
>
> Socrates: Do the orators strike you as speaking always with a view to what is best, with the single aim of making the citizens as good as possible by their speeches, or are they, like the poets, set on gratifying the citizens, and do they, sacrificing the common-weal to their own interest, behave to these assemblies as to children, trying merely to gratify them, nor care a jot whether they will be better or worse in consequence?[50]

Thus, it would seem that Socrates viewed the poetic enterprise as an irresponsible endeavor. Its effect on the citizenry was wholly negative and in fact highly destructive. Its only accomplishment was the undermining of character. "In the Gorgias for instance, it is taken for granted that tragedy aims only at the gratification of pleasure (hedone), and it is, therefore, characterized as an adulatory art (kolakeia) whose objective cannot be genuine virtue (arete)."[51] It can be seen from the statement of Snell and from the analysis of dialogues that preceded this statement that Plato viewed the work and influence of the poet in an extremely negative fashion. As a result Nietzsche's contention that with the advent of Socrates, the poetic was forced into suppression or exile appears to be initially plausible. However, from the first appearance of The Birth of Tragedy to the present, there have been various attempts to save Plato and Socrates from the harsh blows of Nietzsche. The question is,

---

50. Plato, Plato, Lysis, Symposium, Gorgias, (502B), E.Capps, T.E. Page, and W.H.D. Rouse, eds., trans. by W.R.M. Lamb (9 vols.: London, William Heinemann, 1914-1926. New York: G.P. Putnam's Sons, 1914-1926), v. pp. 451-453.

51. Bruno Snell, The Discovery of the Mind, p. 115.

however, whether Plato and Socrates can slip elusively away from their roles as cultural idols and avoid the violent swing of Nietzsche's philosophical hammer. Havelock, in his book Preface to Plato, presents a case that has a great deal of commonality with Nietzsche. In setting the context for a discussion of the scholars who have attempted to explain Plato's harsh renunciation of poetry, Havelock tries to expose Plato's position in its most acute form:

> Let us for a moment consider further the tone and temper of Plato's attack. He opens by characterizing the effect of poetry as 'a crippling of the mind.' It is a kind of disease, for which one has to acquire an antidote . . . In short, poetry is a species of mental poison, and is the enemy of truth. This is surely a shocker to the sensibilities of any modern reader and his incredulity is not lessened by the peroration with which, a good many pages later, Plato winds up his argument: 'Crucial indeed is the struggle, more crucial than we think--the choice that makes us good or bad--to keep faithful to righteousness and virtue in the face of temptation, be it of fame or money or power, or of poetry--yes, even of poetry.' If he thus exhorts us to fight the good fight against poetry, like a Greek Saint Paul warring against the powers of darkness, we can conclude either that he has lost all sense of proportion, or that his target cannot be poetry in our sense, but something more fundamental in the Greek experience, and more powerful... Plato's target seems to be precisely the poetic experience as such. It is an experience we would characterize as aesthetic. To him it is a kind of psychic poison. You must always have your antidote ready. He seems to want to destroy poetry as poetry,to exclude her as a vehicle of communication. He is not just attacking bad poetry or extravagant poetry. This is made even clearer during the course of the argument he builds against her.[52]

---

52. Eric A. Havelock, Preface to Plato (Oxford: Basil Blackwell, 1963), pp. 4-5.

Havelock is here making it clear that Plato is not merely against "bad poets" but against poetic communication as such. This we find to be valid in view of what we have observed in the *Republic*, *Apology*, and *Gorgias*. The argument of Plato's that we have reviewed concerning the comparison of the poet and artist can serve as an example. It is not merely the "bad poet" that Plato is describing; it is poetic activity and experience itself. Yet, in the face of this there arise attempts to help Plato and Socrates slip away. Havelock contends that this results from an unwillingness or reluctance to take Plato at face value and "when they reach a context like the present they start looking around for an escape hatch."[53] Havelock then goes on to trace the various escape hatches that have been employed.

The first of these centers around the activity of the questioning Socrates. Socrates talked with the poets, and as we have seen previously, attempted to discover the nature of their work. He has asked the poets to give a rational explanation of their work and its contents. Thus, he gave the poet a chance to defend himself:

> . . . has he not said that poetry may offer a defense of herself if she can? Has he not confessed to her overpowering charms? Does he not admit reluctance to expel her, and does this not mean that in effect he recants? He does indeed so confess, but to think that his confession amounts to a recantation profoundly mistakes his intention. Indeed, the terms in which he makes the concession to poetry, to plead her case if she chooses, are themselves damning. For he treats her in effect as a kind of prostitute, or as a Delilah who may seduce Plato's Samson if he lets her, and so rob him of his strength. She can charm and coax and wheedle and enthral, but these are precisely the powers that are so fatal. If we listen, we dare to do so only as we counter her spell with one of our own.[54]

---

53. *Ibid.*, p. 4

54. *Ibid.*, pp. 4-5.

Yes, Socrates would listen to the poet, but would not the defense of rationality ultimately destroy what the poet had said? If the poet could not state his case in a way that fit Socrates' demand for rationality, then the poet must be excluded because his mysterious and unintelligible tirades must not be allowed to destroy the purity of the rational soul. This is clearly in tune with Nietzsche's insights. In Götzen-Dammerung Nietzsche refers to reason as a tyrant that works as a counter tyrant to "counter the dark desires with a permanent daylight--the daylight of reason."[55] Socrates is thus willing to play with the poets in their defense of poetry, but would ultimately crush them with the tyranny of reason.

Another attempt to salvage Plato's position on poetry makes an appeal to the literary ability of Plato himself:

> Was not the master a great poet himself, commanding a style which if it chose could abandon abstract argument in order to appeal to all the resources of the imagination either by vivid portraiture or by symbolic myth? Could a writer of such sensitive prose have really been indifferent nay hostile, to the rhythmic arrangement and the verbal imagery which are secrets of the poetic style? No, he must have been ironic or temporarily petulant. He cannot, surely, have meant what he said. The attack on poetry can and must be explained away, cut down to size, rendered inocuous enough to fit our conception of what Platonism stands for.[56]

This evasive technique reminds us immediately of Nietzsche's description of his philosophizing in the area of cultural idols. Viewing Socrates and Plato as cultural idols would mean that the idols, Plato and Socrates, must at all cost be preserved. Operating behind this is an acute tension. One aspect of this tension

---

55. Friedrich Nietzsche, Nietzsche's Werke, VIII, p. 74. Translation mine.

> ". . . gegen die dunklen Begehrungen ein Tageslicht in Permanenz herstellen--das Tageslicht der Vernunft."

56. Eric A. Havelock, Preface to Plato, pp. 6-7.

is the "modern taste for poetry."[57] This refers to the value that is placed on poetry because the modern intellect,to a great extent,affirms its value. On the other hand, Plato and Socrates with their cult of rationalism have enjoyed longevity on the western Olympus. Plato and Socrates must be salvaged and poetry must not be exiled. The way out of this dilemma is simply to say that Plato did not mean what he said. This option would be plausible if Plato would have made only a statement in passing concerning the poets. But clearly this is not the case. Plato has Socrates state the case against poetry with too much rigor and thoroughness for us to pass it off as merely jesting.

Another escape route accepts the argument that Plato definitely wanted to exclude poets from the society he was describing. But then "Plato is accommodated to modern taste by arguing that the exclusion of poetry applies only to an ideal condition not realizable in the recognizable future or in earthly societies."[58] Is the society that Plato describes in the Republic really so far from realization in historical actuality? Havelock thinks not: "The reforms which are proposed are considered urgent in the present and are not utopian."[59] This contention of Havelock seems to be correct in view of two kinds of evidence. First of all, according to the description of Plato in the Gorgias, the Apology, and the Republic, Socrates spent at least part of his time engaged in dialogues that were specifically directed against poets. Socrates tried to show that their activity was not understandable to reason and therefore ridiculous, and not virtuous. If poetry was to be excluded only from the ideal state why does Socrates try to drive it from the Athens that he inhabitated? The second kind of evidence arises out of Friedländer's analysis of one of Plato's autobiographical letters. From Friedländer's analysis of this letter it can be seen that Plato was deeply concerned with the immediate political and societal conditions of his environment. It was for this reason that he frequented the circle of Socrates. He hoped to find an answer through philosophizing and philosophical discourse that could be implemented to change the conditions of his age. Friedländer contends that Plato's ultimate goal was that of correcting the political situation in Athens and on his journey to securing this goal Plato established his philosophy. "He set out in quest of

---

57. Ibid., p. 7.

58. Ibid.

59. Ibid.

the best state and on this quest discovered the world of the forms."[60] It would seem from Havelock's contention and the evidence of Friedländer that Plato and Socrates' concern was with the present and not with some ideal and abstract state which they knew would never come into existence or actualization. Socrates' concern was immediate and pointed. His criticism was directed against the Athens he frequented. His concern was focused in a criticism of the poet who in Socrates' time,was the dominant cultural and educational influence.

In turning to other studies of Greek culture and the origin of philosophy written during the years following the publications of Nietzsche, there developed a significant trend in Greek studies that was antagonistic to the contentions of Nietzsche. This trend began with Wilamowitz-Moellendorf,who offered a severe and harsh criticism of The Birth of Tragedy as soon as it was published. This initial criticism of Nietzsche was by no means Wilamowitz's most significant contribution and,as Walter Kaufmann contends this criticism was entirely blind to the merits of The Birth of Tragedy.[61] Wilamowitz's Der Glaube der Hellenen differs radically in tone and form from his early criticism of Nietzsche. It is sound and extremely scholarly; it also lacks the anger and vehemence that was the essence of his early criticisms of Nietzsche. Der Glaube der Hellenen binds together Wilamowitz's most significant contribution to Greek studies and is for the greater part regarded as his most significant work. In this work Wilamowitz initiates a trend in Greek scholarship that emphasizes the continuity of Greek religion in Greek philosophy. Jaeger summarizes Wilamowitz's contention as follows: "Wilamowitz, in his posthumous work Der Glaube der Hellenen, . . . has given the Greek philosophers a place in the religious development of the Greek people."[62] Jaeger is congenial to this thesis,but is not satisfied with Wilamowitz's development of it. He contends that Wilamowitz's study was stunted by his Protestant bias and as a result Wilamowitz was unable to see the fullness of religious meaning in the work of the Greek philosophers. It is not the present task to defend or destroy this criticism that Jaeger wages at Wilamowitz but it is

---

60. Paul Friedländer, Plato, An Introduction, trans. by Hans Meyerhoff (3rd ed.; New York and Evanston: Harper & Row, 1958), p.6.

61. Walter Kaufmann, Nietzsche, pp. 34-35.

62. Werner Jaeger, The Theology of the Early Greek Philosophers (Oxford: Clarendon Press, 1947), p. s.

important to recognize that Jaeger consciously places himself in the tradition of Wilamowitz:

> So one of our primary aims must be to give the religion of the philosophers--and not only that of the pre-Socratic thinkers--a really positive place in our effort to understand how Greek religion developed. . . I long ago started my work on pre-Socratic philosophy under such men as Hermann Diels and Wilamowitz and I am bound to approach it as a part of the history of the Greek genius.[63]

An example can serve to illustrate the way this thesis finds expression. The example is this: "The philosophical idea of God from the apeiron to the Nous is undeniably accompanied by an increasing resemblance to Zeus."[64] This is to say that mythological conceptions were not banished in the emergence of rational philosophy but that they were appropriated and transformed and thus the religious tradition of the Greeks found continuity, not death, in the embrace of philosophical concepts. The gods of Greece were not exiled, but were given a different form in the philosophical mind of the pre-Socratics and Socrates.

In F.M. Cornford's From Religion to Philosophy: A Study in the Origin of Western Speculation basically the same thesis is developed. Cornford describes the era with which he is concerned as the moment in history when rational inquiry asserted its supremacy in the arena of ultimate things. This arena had previously been dominated by traditional belief. This assertion of rational supremacy for Cornford did not mark a severe break with the ways of thought that preceded it:

> There is a real continuity between the earliest rational speculation and the religious representation that lay behind it; . . . Philosophy inherited from religion certain great conceptions--for instance, the ideas of 'God,' 'Soul,' 'Destiny,' 'Law,'--which continued to circumscribe the movements of rational thought and to determine their main directions. Religion expresses itself in poetical symbols and in terms of mythical personalities; Philosophy prefers the language of dry

---

63. Ibid., pp. 8-9.

64. Ibid., p. 174.

> abstraction, and speaks of substance, cause, matter, and so forth. But the outward difference only disguises an inward and substantial affinity between these two successive products of the same consciousness. The modes of thought that attain to clear definition and explicit statement in philosophy were already implicit in the unreasoned intuitions of mythology.[65]

Cornford proceeds to substantiate this thesis in a very thorough and scholarly way. It is not insignificant that Cornford, as did Jaeger, sees Zeus being transformed into philosophical form. Cornford contends that in a mythical way Plato "amplifies and reinterprets" the doctrine of Anaxagoras,which is that reason brought about order and distinction and separated all things which were formerly confounded together. Reason thus takes the place of Zeus, but the activity and function of reason and Zeus are the same; it is to bring order and distinction into a confounded and confused situation. Plato saw the task of his generation of philosophers to restore this order that had been established by Zeus. As Cornford suggests, this for Plato was not to be accomplished by violence or force but by the power and clarity of reason.

Cornford carefully develops his case and by no means limits his analysis to Zeus and his counterpart reason. He continues to push his thesis forward and argues that Plato's philosophy of the forms is basically a mythological phenomenon with a great deal of religious meaning and content transformed into it. Thus, for Cornford, it is not a purely philosophical projection. This is to say that Plato's theory of the forms has a definite place in the religious development of the Greek people. It is part of the mythological tradition that, according to Cornford(as it was for Jaeger and Wilamowitz),continues uninterrupted in Greek philosophy.

Cornford, in Principium Sapientiae: The Origins of Greek Philosophical Thought, develops this thesis in yet another way. Here Cornford argues that the philosopher assumes the role that the Seer-Poet had previously held. The philosopher became the contact with the divine and thus he became the "religious" leader of Greece. This did not begin with Plato, but Cornford contends it was already present in the pre-Socratics:

---

65. F.M. Cornford, From Religion to Philosophy: A Study in the Origins of Western Speculation (New York: Harper & Row, 1957), p. v.

> Pythagoreanism was a philosophy as well as a religion. Philosophically, the truth contemplated is the ultimate nature of things; religiously, it is the knowledge which enables man to advance to spiritual perfection, by assimilating his own nature to the unseen order of the world... Pythagoras was regarded as a prophet of the mantic Apollo and the hierophant of a sacred revelation. The content of the revelation is the intellectual truths of mathematics, apprehended by the reason, not given in everyday sensible experience. The rational soul (τὸ λογικὸν ἔχον), in this dualistic system, is the divine, immortal element in our nature, opposed to the passions and senses of the body. The knowledge gained in contemplation comes from that other world of gods and spirits which the soul visits when detached from the body in concentrated thought, and still more when it is set free by death. The fallen soul thus regains its divinity; man becomes godlike by assimilating his moral nature to the harmonious order the intellect reveals.[66]

Cornford also argues that this is the case for Heraclitus and Parmenides. Heraclitus, according to Cornford, claimed to possess a unique inspiration that resulted from a search of himself and his being. This inspiration took form and could be shared when Heraclitus spoke. When he spoke, either verbally or through his aphorisms, the _logos_ became manifest and he asked his readers to listen, not to him, but to the _logos_.[67] The _logos_, if apprehended, would give the individual a unified picture of the world and the truth contained in this apprehension was a religious message far superior to the variety of ideas that the poets and the oracles taught. Heraclitus, according to his own conviction, was the vehicle for a truth that superseded all other truth. Heraclitus was thus in the religious tradition of the oracle and the poet who were vehicles for messages from the divine.

Parmenides also saw himself as a vehicle for revelation. His message was imparted to him by a goddess. According to Cornford, "she is unquestionably the goddess of Reason, a projection of that

---

66. F.M. Cornford, _Principium Sapientiae: The Origins of Greek Philosophical Thought_, ed. by W.K.C. Guthrie (New York: Harper & Row, 1965), pp. 111-112.

67. _Ibid._, p. 113.

faculty which is exercised in mathematical reasoning, deducing certain conclusions from self-evident principles."[68] The message that reason gave is described in this way by Cornford:

> Parmenides' originality lies in his perception that there is a gulf, which cannot be bridged, between that realm of timeless, metaphysical truth and the welter of changing qualities which the senses, and the opinions of mortals founded on the senses, falsely mistake for realities. Henceforth the immortal and divine element in man is no longer merely the spirit which, when it leaves the sleeping body, communes with gods in prophetic dreams and visions and discerns the course of past, present, and future time; it has become the faculty which thinks and gives a rational account of metaphysical reality beyond the boundaries of time and change. Parmenides, however, remains a prophet, since his entire discourse is revealed to him by inspiration. In other words, he has this much in common with Heraclitus, that he feels his discourse to be, not merely what he says and believes, but the truth.[69]

Cornford gives further evidence for his case by saying that Parmenides was following the tradition that believed that poetry was the language of revelation. Cornford also suggests that Parmenides wishes to give his ideas poetic form so that they could easily be committed to memory. Memory was central to the oral religious traditions that preceded him. Memory was the main vehicle that Parmenides hoped to employ in propagating his ideas.

After describing briefly how Parmedides fit into the tradition of Greek religion, Cornford proceeds to Socrates. Socrates does not seem to slide into the categories that Cornford established with the ease that he was able to manipulate Heraclitus and Parmenides. In fact, Cornford seemed to be satisfied with leaving Socrates standing outside the categories of religion into which he has placed Heraclitus and Parmenides. Socrates had no message

---

68. Ibid., p. 120.

69. Ibid., p. 120.

to impart and did not see himself as the religious paragon of his era. He claimed to know nothing and to give nothing; he only could help men find what they had already known but could not recollect. This project was not a phenomenon that was a gift of the gods or inspired by the gods; it was the pursuit of human perfection.

According to Cornford, this is the case for the historical Socrates and "It is only in Plato's middle dialogues that Socrates first takes on, in addition to his real character, the poetical or prophetic traits needed for the full disclosure of the Platonic revelation."[70] Plato in this view is making a definite movement beyond Socrates. The metaphysical message that Plato wanted to give could not be expressed in the completely rational language of the prosaic Socrates. Plato experienced the need to go beyond the posture of the midwife and find a vehicle for his message. Cornford describes this movement beyond Socrates in this way:

> As we have seen, the religious belief in immortality carried Plato beyond the rational agnosticism of Socrates, truthfully reproduced in the _Apology_. As a consequence, in the middle dialogues from the _Gorgias_ onwards, poetical myth appears as a distinct element alongside of the dialectical argument inherited from Socrates. In both elements it is the highest part of the soul that is at work. In the myth it exercises the old mantic power of prophetic vision, formerly attributed to the soul when it leaves the body in sleep, 'free to reach out, in its pure and independent condition, to perceive some new knowledge of things past, present, or to come' (_Rep_.527A). Thus Plato the philosopher resumes the role of prophet and poet which Socrates had disclaimed, although, by keeping dialectic and myth apart, Plato acknowledged his master's distinction between truth that can be established as knowledge by rational argument and truth that can only be divined and must remain a matter for belief and persuasion.[71]

Plato, according to Cornford, took up a role that Socrates had disclaimed. He projected a myth and made his contributions to the religious history of Greece. The realm of the divine which formerly could be contacted through the poet and oracle now became the source and goal of the philosopher's knowledge.

---

70. _Ibid_., p. 125.

71. _Ibid_., p. 126.

The trend in Greek scholarship that has been described in the preceding paragraphs is of extreme importance when it is brought to bear on the insights of Nietzsche. If there is real and comprehensive continuity between the Greek religions that preceded Greek philosophy, and Greek Philosophy itself, then it would seem that there is a significant point of view that is contrary to Nietzsche's insights and contentions. Nietzsche contended that the Greek imagination flowed freely and creatively until the advent of the prosaic Socrates. Socrates with the tyranny of reason disrupted and destroyed the creative dimension in Greek culture. This resulted from reason forcing the exile of the Dionysian, that is, the exile of the dark, the mysterious, and the chaotic. It was through the free interplay of the intellect or form giving realities with the dark and mysterious dimension that the Greek imagination received its sustenance for creative activity. If the Greek genius was not stunted or interrupted, but merely given different form, then to claim, as Nietzsche does, that the origin of rational philosophy destroyed the Greek genius would seem at least to be highly questionable.

It is therefore necessary to evaluate the conflict of these contentions and to see if Nietzsche's insights can surpass this conflict. This can be examined in terms of if and how the mysterious and the freely imaginative is appropriated in Plato. This will involve a testing to see if the Dionysian is in any way integrated into Socratic and Platonic philosophy or if, as Nietzsche contended, it is exiled and as a result thought is torn from a interplay with the dark and mysterious. This will involve eliciting the crucial assumptions of Nietzsche and Plato concerning the nature of reason and reality, and also to expose these assumptions and employ them in illuminating the problem.

At this point the study at hand must be pushed beyond a defense of Nietzsche, and the problem laid bare by exposing the conflict between Nietzsche and Plato. It may be the case that the central thrust of Nietzsche's insights concerning the origin and effect of reason is defensible. At this point, however, viewing the problem through the insights of Nietzsche must be suspended. Exploring the conflict of crucial assumptions between Nietzsche and Plato and through the analysis of this conflict allows aspects of Plato's thought to be seen somewhat independently of the insights of Nietzsche. Discussing the conflict of crucial assumptions hopefully will bring this study to greater clarity, accuracy, and objectivity. This conflict has already appeared in a basic disagreement concerning the work of the poet. Nietzsche saw the exiling of the poetic as definite evidence for the tyranny of reason in its confrontation with the mysterious. It does seem evident that Plato and Socrates did want to drive out the tragic poet. It is also clear that Socrates, as he is seen through Plato, destroys the work of the poet through the tyranny of his rational dialogue. It is now necessary to see if the mysterious and the poetic assume a different form in Plato and Socrates' philosophies and if the reality and the effect of the poetic and the mysterious are retained.

CHAPTER III

PLATO, SOCRATES, AND MYSTERY

"Reason is like a monarch who, when he comes to power, determines to disregard those provinces which he feels he cannot rule effectively and to concentrate on those which he is sure he can control."

Paul Hazard

In describing the posture that Plato assumed concerning the mysterious, the thesis must be explored whether or not it is necessary to differentiate in this matter between Socrates and Plato. Nietzsche, in The Birth of Tragedy, seemed to direct his passionate comments largely against Socrates. This was also the case in Philosophy in the Tragic Age of the Greeks and Twilight of the Idols. Nietzsche contended, however, that the poetic career of Plato was disrupted and destroyed when the young poet encountered the prosaic Socrates. Given that this was the case, then the harshly rational aspects of Plato's thought would be attributed to the influence of his teacher Socrates. Even though Nietzsche suggested that the youthful Plato was influenced by Socrates, Nietzsche did not contend that this gives us a reason to crucially discriminate between the philosophy of Socrates and the philosophy of Plato. He treated them as if their philosophies possessed a definite similarity. In the following example, in which he acknowledges the influence of Socrates on Plato but does not differentiate their thought, this can be seen.

> But to Socrates it seemed that tragic art did not even "tell the truth;" moreover, it addressed itself to "those who are not very bright, not to the philosopher; a twofold reason for shunning it. Like Plato, he reckoned it among the flattering arts which portray only the agreeable, not the useful; and therefore he required of his disciples abstinence and strict separation from such unphilosophical attractions--with such success that the youthful tragic poet Plato first burned his poems that he might become a student of Socrates.[72]

It is crucial to acknowledge that Nietzsche treats Socrates and Plato's thought as essentially similar. Nietzsche proceeds almost unreflectingly, assuming that this is the case. In the present exposition of Nietzsche's insights the same position has been assumed. Socrates has been viewed through the works of Plato, i.e., their positions have been regarded as possessing an essential continuity and similarity. What might be distinctively Platonic and what might have been distinctively Socratic has not been differentiated.

In the preceding discussion of Wilamowitz, Cornford, and Jaeger, it has been seen that these men contended that Greek philosophy was essentially part of the development of Greek religion. Cornford in developing this position claims that the

---

72. Friedrich Nietzsche, The Birth of Tragedy, p. 90.

historical Socrates does not fit into this development of Greek religion.[73] Plato, according to Cornford, transformed Socrates to fit his purposes and uses Socrates to propagate his mythical message. This is to say that only in Socrates does one confront the prosaic and the rational. Plato was temporarily influenced by Socrates but transcended this influence and instituted the mythical tradition by means of his vision of the forms. Cornford couches this contention in what he calls a distinction between the early and the late dialogues. This is a distinction that he describes as commonly accepted:

> The last and greatest attempt to formulate the mystical faith in rational terms was made by Plato. . . Platonism, if we take it to mean principally the theory of Forms or 'Ideas,' will turn out to belong to the mystic tradition.
>
> It is now generally agreed that we may distinguish a group of early dialogues, commonly called 'Socratic,' from a later group in which the doctrines characteristic of Orphism and Pythagoreanism for the first time made their appearance. Typical of the Socratic group are the _Apology_, _Laches_, _Charmides_, and other minor dialogues, written within ten years after the death of Socrates (399 B.C.). The mystical group, heralded by the _Gorgias_, included the _Meno_, _Symposium_, _Phaedo_, _Republic_, _Phaedrus_. It is held that the _Gorgias_ was composed shortly before or after 387 B.C., the year when Plato, at the age of forty, set up his school at the Academy. Before he thus settled at Athens, Plato, who went abroad after the death of Socrates, had almost certainly spent some time with the Megarian Socratics, and also travelled in Sicily, where Pythagorean thought must have survived the dispersion of the communities. We have every reason to connect the change of tone and of doctrine from the Socratic to the mystic group with these opportunities of contact with Pythagoreanism, a type of philosophy which seems to have been little known to the Athens of Plato's youth.[74]

The mystical or mythological side of Plato's thinking Cornford attributes to the influence of Plato's contact with Pythagoreanism. The early and harshly rational aspects of Plato's thought Cornford

---

73. F.M. Cornford, _Principium Sapientiae,_ pp. 124-25.

74. F.M. Cornford, _From Religion to Philosophy_, pp. 242-43.

ascribes to the influence of Socrates. The dialogues that employ myths as a device of explanation and assume a somewhat favorable posture concerning the poetic and the mysterious are those that fall under the period of Pythagorean influence. The dialogues that are harshly prosaic and exhibit only the tight dialectic are regarded as being crucially influenced by Socrates. Through this means the poetic and mystical aspects are placed in their allegedly correct context. To evaluate this contention Plato's apprehension of the mysterious shall be examined. This will be accomplished by exploring the mystical or mythological aspects of his thought and trying to see if there is a crucial difference between the two facets of Plato's thought which Cornford described as the Socratic and the Pythagorean. The crucial difference to be tested for is whether reason assumes a different role in the mystical aspects of Plato or if its role is essentially the same in the so-called Pythagorean period and in the Socratic period. After exposing Plato's posture concerning reason and mystery Nietzsche's insights will be examined once again to see if these insights fully take into account this facet of Plato's thought. The attempt will be made to see if Plato's description of Socrates' apprehension of the mysterious invalidates Nietzsche's contention that with the advent of Socrates, reason rose to a position of tyranny and that the dark, mysterious, and poetic were banished.

The first aspect of Plato and Socrates' thought that would at least initially seem to be evidence for their apprehension and recognition of the poetic, mystical, and the mysterious is the phenomenon which Plato describes as Socrates' daimon. In the Apology, Plato, in his description of Socrates, treats the daimon as something beyond Socrates' control. Friedländer describes the role the daimon plays in this way:

> Plato first introduced the daimonion into his portrait of Socrates as a trait just as characteristic of this strange man as his turned-up nose and protruding eyes. Socrates himself says in his speech of defense that it appeared frequently and opposed him even in trifles (Apology 40A). . . we are told in the Euthydemus (272E) that the 'sign of the demon' prevents him from rising, thus causing his encounter with the quarrelsome fencing masters. We are even less surprised when, in the Phaedrus, the sign does not permit him to leave before he has made amends to Eros with another and more truthful speech (242C).[75]

---

75. Paul Friedländer, Plato, p. 34.

Friedländer proceeds to portray the role of the _daimon_ in Socrates' activity by examples from the _Theages_, _Alcibiades_ and _Theaetetus_. In each case the _daimon_ seems to be able, at times, to assert absolute control over Socrates and forces him to act or refrain from acting.

Socrates, who sought to bring all of his life and thought under the clear and solid control of reason, was at times forced by the _daimon_ to act against his will. Thus it would seem that there was an aspect of Socrates' being that broke the tyranny of his rationality. In testing to see if this is the case, it is necessary to look more closely at the function of the _daimon_ in Socrates' life and see how it relates to what Socrates describes as the controlling element of the soul.

One of the most insightful understandings of the Socratic _daimon_ is found in _Plutarch's Moralia_. In Plutarch's understanding, this type of _daimon_ is found only in persons of a special character. The purest of persons with the most highly developed rational capacities are the only persons that possess and are possessed by this type of _daimon_. This _daimon_ allows for special apprehension and understanding:

> But whereas some men actually have this sort of apprehension in dreams, hearing better asleep, when the body is quiet and undisturbed, while when they are awake their soul can hear the higher powers but faintly, and moreover, as they are overwhelmed by the tumult of their passions and the distractions of their wants, they cannot listen or attend to the message; Socrates, on the other hand, had an understanding which, being pure and free from passion, and commingling with the body but little, for necessary ends, was so sensitive and delicate as to respond at once to what reached him. What reached him, one would conjecture, was not spoken language, but the unuttered words of a daemon, making voiceless contact with his intelligence by their sense alone.[76]

---

76. Plutarch, _Plutarch's Moralia_, (588D and E), T.E. Page _et al._, eds., trans. by Phillip H. DeLacy and Benedict Einarson (15 vols.;(London: William Heinemann, Ltd., 1927-1967. Cambridge, Mass.: Harvard University Press, 1927-1967), VII, p. 451.

Friedländer assigns a great deal of significance to this interpretation and calls it "profound." In this interpretation a possible explanation for the relationship between the *daimon* and the rational soul can be found.

> In Plutarch's dialogue *About the Daimonion of Socrates*, a childishly crude confusion of the Socratic daimonion with such phenomena as sneezing or as soothsaying "voices," used for the purposes of popular diviniation, is replaced by a more profound view. . . as human speech affects the ear, so the *Logoi* (to retain this equivocal term) of the demons directly affect the human soul. What ordinary people experience only in the relaxation of sleep is given to human beings with a pure, serene soul--whom we then call holy or demonic--in their waking lives. Such a human being, free from disharmony and turmoil, was Socrates... that is, the purest part of the reason (*vous*) in especially favored individuals, the part that is excluded from the mingling of soul and body. As the corks float above the net, so the demonic star floats above the human being, and his soul is fastened to it, whether willingly or reluctantly. .... According to the *Timaeus*, the god gives to everybody a demon as part of his soul. Its seat is the head, which is akin to heaven and, therefore, raised toward it. And this divine element (τὸ θεῖον) must be cultivated so that man keeps the demon in an orderly habitat, and becomes "eudaemonic." What, from a logical and psychological point of view, is called reason is here reverently related to the highest form of existence. With this "doctine" of the *Timaeus*, Plutarch appears to have combined what Plato wrote about the demon in the myths of the soul. ... Thus the demon is, in Plato's world, a symbol not only for that which Goethe respected as a special power, "*So musst du sein*" (*Unworte*, ΔΑΙΜΩΝ), but also for the mysterious and inexorable bond between human life and the beyond.
>
> . . . .
>
> We are also reminded of the myth of the soul in the *Republic*, where judgment is passed at a "demonic" place "between" heaven and earth (X 614C); and of the faint echo in the *Timaeus* (90A), where the demon, the controlling element in the soul, "lifts us from earth to kinship in heaven." ... And the more sharply Plato's world was divided into idea and appearance, the stronger must be the bond forcing this separation into a unity. ... Without the proportion of the elements, without the harmonious

system of the forms of being and knowledge, without the *metaxy* of the soul, without the realm of the "demonic," heaven and earth would break asunder.[77]

The daimon in this view is given to the most rational of persons and is this person's crucial link with the world of the forms. It is not a capacity that is overtly irrational, but it is a capacity that enables the purest of individuals to be occasionally in complete contact with the forms. It frees him from the stifling effects of the body and allows him to participate more fully in the realm of the spiritual. In the *Timaeus* we find this to be the case. Here the daimon is the guiding and directing part of the soul:

> As concerning the most sovereign form of soul in us we must conceive that heaven has given it to each man as a guiding genius--that part which we say dwells in the summit of the body and lifts us from earth toward our celestial affinity, like a plant whose roots are not in earth, but in the heavens.[78]

In this translation Cornford refers to the *daimon* as a guiding "genius." In the translation of the *Timaeus* by R.G. Bury, *daimon* appears instead of genius.[79] The Greek ΔΑΙΜΩΝ to which the two translations refer is difficult to render without ambiguity. *Daimon* appears as demon in English and carries a negative connotation, that is, it is usually viewed as an undesirable or "evil" spirit. Genius in English refers to a superior intellect that is only possessed by a very few extremely creative people. Neither of these meanings capture the reality that Plato is attempting to convey. Friedländer, commenting on the *Timaeus*, gives us an extremely helpful insight into the meaning of the word *daimon*. Friedländer contends that in Plato's view everyone has *a daimon* that is part of his soul. It is man's duty to cultivate *this daimon* so that it becomes orderly and useful, or "eudaemonic." This, according to Friedländer, is none other than reason, which

---

77. Paul Friedländer, *Plato*, pp. 37-38, 42-43.

78. Plato, *Plato's Timaeus*, (90a), Oskar Piest, ed., trans. by Francis M. Cornford (New York: The Liberal Arts Press, 1959), p. 114.

79. Plato, *Plato, Timaeus, Cleitophon, Critias, Menexenus, Epistles*, (90a), T.E. Page, E. Capps, W.H.D. Rouse, eds., trans. by R.G. Bury (London: William Heinemann, Ltd., 1914-1926. New York: G.P. Putnam's Sons, 1914-1926), VII, p. 245.

is the highest part of the soul. If man cultivates this aspect of his soul to the extent that Socrates did then his life could be pure, orderly and virtuous. It is not insignificant that this part of the soul is the bond between the human life and the life beyond. The daimon, the controlling element of the soul, or the cultivated rational capacity, connects the mortal man with the eternal world of the forms. It was this aspect of his being that originated in the world of the forms and will in death return to the world of the forms. The daimon of Socrates, in view of Plato's description, Plutarch's insights, and Friedländer's commentary, would be none other than the highly cultivated rational part of Socrates' soul. It would not be an irrational facet of Socrates' life that buffeted him about with no coherent meaning. It was a pure contact with the forms that in a particular situation would compel him to act or refrain from acting or, as in the Phaedrus (242c), to make amends by giving a more truthful speech. Dodds views the daimon in essentially the same way. He contends:

> Eventually Plato picked up and completely transformed the idea, as he did with so many elements of popular belief: the daemon becomes a sort of lofty spirit-guide, or Freudian Superego, who in the Timaeus is identified with the element of pure reason in man.[80]

Dodds' description of the daimon is thus in tune with Plato, Plutarch, Cornford, and Friedländer. The daimon is not a source of mystery, chaos, and irrationality, but is the highest capacity of the rational soul. This seems to be clearly in agreement with Nietzsche's contentions:

> Dionysus had already been scared from the tragic stage, by a demonic power speaking through Euripides. Even Euripides was, in a sense, only a mask: the deity that spoke through him was neither Dionysus nor Apollo, but an altogether newborn demon, called Socrates.
>
> . . . .
>
> We are offered a key to the character of Socrates by the wonderful phenomenon known as "the daimonion of Socrates." In exceptional circumstances, when his tremendous intellect wavered, he found secure support in the utterances of a divine voice that spoke up at such moments.[81]

---

80. E.R. Dodds, The Greeks and the Irrational (Berkeley and Los Angeles: University of California Press, 1966) pp. 42-43.

81. Friedrich Nietzsche, The Birth of Tragedy, pp. 82, 88.

The Socratic daimon was the daimon of rationality. It was this daimon according to Nietzsche, that crucially influenced Euripides and that banished the mystery and darkness of Greek tragedy. It was this daimon that forced Dionysus into exile and disrupted the creative interplay between mystery and form or Dionysus and Apollo.

The discussion of Socrates and Plato's integration of irrationality and mystery cannot end here for there is another facet of Plato's description of Socrates that seems to be a means through which they apprehended mystery and irrationality. This possible source for mystery and irrationality is referred to as "divine madness." In the Phaedrus Socrates contends that "we owe our greatest blessing to madness."[82] It seems blatantly paradoxical, if not contradictory, that the severely rational Socrates would contend that this is the case. Is it possible that "divine madness" is a phenomenon that Nietzsche did not take into consideration when he claimed that in Socrates we find the tyranny of the rational? Does not Socrates in his statement on the "blessings of madness" clearly demonstrate that he did not allow reason to reach a position of complete tyranny? To see if Nietzsche's insights break down at this point and do not account for this facet of Socrates, it is necessary to take a closer look at what the phenomenon of "divine madness" signified for Socrates, that is, for the Socrates we see through the works of Plato.

To come to some understanding of the phenomenon of divine madness, a look at a work that deals specifically with this subject is appropriate. This work is Josef Pieper's Enthusiasm and Divine Madness, which is a study of the Platonic dialogue Phaedrus. In this work Pieper contends that the phenomenon of "divine madness" is the central problem of the dialogue. "The greatest blessings come by way of mania, insofar as mania is heaven-sent. This pronouncement of Socrates unquestionably forms the very heart of the whole dialogue."[83] Pieper then proceeds in a most helpful and scholarly fashion to describe this "blessing":

---

82. Plato, The Phaedrus, Lysis, and Protagoras of Plato, (244a), J. Wright, ed., (London: Macmillan and Co., Ltd.,1916), p. 43.

83. Josef Pieper, Enthusiasm and Divine Madness on the Platonic Dialogue Phaedrus, trans. by Richard and Clara Winston (New York: Harcourt, Brace, and World, Inc., 1964), p. 47.

> Socrates does not maintain that _mania_ is normal to man and essential to his soundness. Rather, he says that it is not an evil in every case. Nor does he outrightly declare _mania_ a good. Instead, he says that it can possibly be a means, an aid, a path to a good, in fact even to the greatest blessings--on condition, that is, that _mania_ is imparted to man as a divine gift.
>
> But what is meant by _mania_? The word is often translated _frenzy_ or _madness_. But "madness" seems to me an inadequate and misleading definition. In the first place, the word connotes unsoundness and irrationality. In the second place, it gives the impression that Socrates is talking about something from the realm of primitive magic. It suggests ties with the orgiastic Dionysian cults. . . If we consider all the aspects of _mania_ which Plato mentions, we shall have to say that he used the word to mean, primarily, a being-beside-oneself, a loss of command over oneself, surrender of autarchic independence and self-control; a state in which we are not active but passive.[84]

Pieper does not see that irrationality and confrontation with chaos is part of this experience. In this moment of ecstasy the individual lets go of himself and "surrenders to the healing darkness of his own divine origin."[85] The topic of this discussion in the _Phaedrus_ is love, and Socrates seeks to show that the encounter with striking beauty and profound love drives the lover beyond the realm of the sensual into a contemplation of the ideal realities of love and beauty. This he compares with the movement of the philosophical pursuit, that is, the movement from the sensual to the realm of the forms.[86] The experience of _ekstasis_ is intrinsically related to this phenomenon. The individual soul through this experience contacts the realm of the forms from which it originated and to which it will return. Pieper states the relationship between the realm of the forms and _ekstasis_ in the following way:

---

84. _Ibid_., p. 49.

85. _Ibid_., p. 62.

86. Plato, _The Phaedrus, Lysis and Protagoras of Plato_, (249a), p. 52.

> What Plato means is that love, insofar as it is real ekstasis, a stepping out of the narrow circle of the self-concerned ego, a frenzy, mania, is capable of carrying aloft with it even the heaviest burden, for it remembers the holy things it once contemplated.[87]

The experience of ekstasis is thus not a plunge into chaos and unintelligibility. It is an experience that allows a temporary "return" to complete intelligibility or to the source of all knowledge--the realm of the forms. The soul, temporarily liberated from individuality and sensuality, soars in contemplation and ecstasy to the realm of perfection and truth.

Cornford, in Principium Sapientiae, develops a strand of thought that is in agreement with what Pieper contends concerning "divine madness" and the realm of the forms. In discussing the various forms of madness that Plato describ es, Cornford states:

> With these forms of 'divine madness' Plato ranks the madness of the philosopher, rapt by the passion for truth into the region above the visible heavens.
>
> . . . .
>
> We have here the philosophic counterpart of the poet's claim to be inspired by the Muses, and the seer's claim to be possessed by Apollo. The philosopher is entheos in a prosaic and literal sense: his mind is a detached part of the divine mind in Nature. This mind, moreover, is the rational part of him, not the irrational.[88]

The enthusiasm and madness of the philosopher, therefore, does not result from his apprehension of the mysterious, the darkness and the unintelligibility of reality. It results from the philosopher's drive to participate in and to reach the realm of the forms by means of his rational intellect. Socrates, in the Phaedrus, exemplifies this by his passion and concern for a pure and ideal form of love. The ekstasis that results from this experience is not a means of recognizing chaos and mystery but a means of contacting the source of ultimate clarity and intelligibility.

E.R. Dodds, in his work The Greeks and the Irrational, offers a thesis which seems at least initially to be contrary to what has been suggested concerning Plato and Socrates in this essay.

---

87. Josef Pieper, Enthusiasm and Divine Madness on the Platonic Dialogue Phaedrus, p. 47.

88. F.M. Cornford, Principium Sapientiae, pp. 143, 150.

Following and defending the insights of Nietzsche, it has been contended that with the development of Socratic and Platonic philosophy, irrationality, darkness and mystery were repressed and subjugated through the tyranny of reason. Dodds, in attempting to demonstrate how Plato and Socrates did pay attention to irrationality, begins by stating this to be the question of his book:

> Were the Greeks in fact quite so blind to the importance of non-rational factors in man's experience and behavior as is commonly assumed both by their apologists and by their critics? This is the question out of which this book grew.[89]

Dodds proceeds on the basis of this question to designate the various ways in which he sees that Plato and Socrates acknowledged and apprehended mystery and irrationality. The first of these ways he calls "The Blessing of Madness." Dodds designates the various forms of madness to which Plato refers and develops one of these forms which is of particular interest to our study: "There remains Plato's third type of 'divine' madness, the type which he defines as 'possession (κατοκωχη) by the Muses' and declares to be indispensable to the production of the best poetry."[90] This statement would seem to contradict what has been in previous paragraphs seen to be the attitude of Plato towards the poet and the nature of his work. In the *Republic*, the *Gorgias*, and the *Apology*, we saw Plato build a strong case against the poet. In the Republic, Plato wanted to go as far as to exclude the poet from his ideal state. In contrast to this in the *Phaedrus* Socrates admits that the best poetry results from being "possessed by the Muses." In the *Apology* he discredited the poets by saying that they could not give a rational defense for their message. In the *Phaedrus* Socrates accepts the poets as a vehicle for a divine message. Pieper is referring to this passage of the *Phaedrus* as offering an explanation:

> The third form of divine madness of which Socrates speaks is poetic *mania*, the ecstasy which comes from the Muses, which "seizes a tender, virgin soul and stimulates it to

---

89. E.R. Dodds, *The Greeks and the Irrational*, p. 1.

90. *Ibid.*, p. 80.

> rapt, passionate expression." This affirmative statement is followed by a negative dictum: True and great poetry is not possible unless it proceeds from divine madness. Those who want to be poets by skill alone will not receive the consecration. The poetry of the sane is brought to naught by the poetry of madness.
>
> "How can this tribute to poetry... be reconciled with its condemnation in The Republic, where Plato would banish Homer and tragedy from his just state?" This query of Wilamowitz recurs in one form or another throughout the literature on Plato. But perhaps there is no real problem here. Plato always--for example, in the dialogue Meno, written long before The Republic--distinguished the "divine poets" from those who had no right to the epithet. And he apparently placed Homer among those other, non-divine poets because Homer attributed ungodly things to the gods.
>
> True poetry, then, has its origin in divine inspiration; it springs from a state of the soul which is madness rather than sanity, and moreover, a madness that is not produced by wine, poison, or drugs, but by a higher power. Poetry, if it is true poetry, springs from "enthusiasm" in the strict, original sense of the word.[91]

The divine poet was acceptable to the Socrates that Plato depicts in the Phaedrus. This poet must, however, derive his inspiration from a "higher power" and through the experience of enthusiasm. This poet would not allow mystery, darkness and irrationality to be part of his thought but he must be possessed by his apprehension of the realm of the forms. His thought as a result would not be penetrated with mystery and unintelligibility, but he would be a vehicle for divine clarity and intelligibility. The "divine poet" would not be a vehicle for mystery and irrationality,as Dodds contends but he would function as the philosopher and through the purest rationality relate himself to the divine realm of the forms.

Dodds contends that there is another way in which Plato recognized irrationality. Dodds discusses this in a chapter

---

91. Josef Pieper, Enthusiasm and Divine Madness, pp. 62-63. Pieper is quoting Wilamowitz's Platon, p. 376.

entitled "Plato and the Irrational Soul."[92] Dodds locates the origin of irrationality in what is referred to in the *Republic* as the conflict between the parts of the soul: "'the passions of the body' becomes in the *Republic* an internal dialogue between two 'parts of the soul.'"[93] Irrationality arises from the conflict between the higher part of the soul, the rational part, and the lower part, the passions. Dodds does not, however, place this discussion of the soul in correct context. In the *Republic* it is blatantly evident that the higher part of the soul, that is, the rational part, could be cultivated into supremacy. This required that the individual would not be exposed to mysterious and unintelligible phenomena such as the poetry of Greek tragedy and that a rational education would bring the passions into subjugation. Dodds is correct in contending that Plato did recognize irrationality and mystery but he does not sufficiently recognize that Plato sought to subjugate and suppress this phenomenon. It is perplexing that Dodds admits that there are parts to the soul, one of which is rational and one of which is irrational, and then concludes that Plato viewed the soul as an irrational phenomenon. One can agree in part with Dodds and recognize that Plato did acknowledge an irrational aspect in man. However, it should be emphasized in contrast to Dodds' contention that Plato sought to bring the irrational aspect of man into subjugation.

There is another possible way in which Plato acknowledged realities and employed methods that were not strictly rational, and thus may have paid attention to mystery and irrationality. This is Plato's use of myth as a device for interpreting and positing the realm of the forms or the realm of pure *Ideas*. Friedländer suggests that Plato offers a variety of paths to reach his ultimate knowledge.

> To lead to a vision of the Idea and a hint of the highest good is Plato's task. Is this perhaps also the true meaning of his decision to write dialogues? However that may be, the dialogues point in different ways to a final goal. While the *Seventh Letter* suggests briefly a progression (διαγωγή) through four definite

---

92. E.R. Dodds, The Greeks and the Irrational, pp. 207-35.

93. *Ibid*., p. 213.

> stages toward "knowledge of the Fifth," i.e., the highest being, the main works delineate three definite paths. The principal path is described in the Republic, first in the famous image of man originally enchained, then liberated and rising toward the light; later in the interpretation of the simile expressly worked out as the "dialectical path." In the Symposium, the prophetess Diotima reveals the true lover's ascent to eternal beauty, and in the same category belongs the myth of the soul in the Phaedrus, the myth of the winged soul's flight to the realm above the heavens. Finally, the Phaedo praises the separation of the soul from the body, presenting the philosopher's life as a pilgrimage to this goal, and his death as the completion of a life so oriented. These three paths may be called the path of knowledge, and knowledge, in turn, is nothing without love and death, which completes it. Thus the three paths may and must be seen as one.[94]

By means of this quotation it is obvious that there is a crucial continuity of meaning and intent in the various dialogues. Plato, in using the method of dialectic, myth, and a description of the soul, had one essential purpose in mind. This purpose was to bring the individual out of the darkness of confusion into the light of the forms. This illumination consisted of understanding the true nature of the individual soul and the ultimate basis for knowledge. It also involved understanding the crucial relationship between the realm of the forms and the soul. Cornford, referring to the Apology, describes this crucial relationship in this way:

> There is a supersensible world, to which soul 'by herself' and the objects of true knowledge belong; and there is the sensible world of body, and of visible and tangible things. The world of the body is a prison, or a tomb; that other world of the soul and of Ideas is the realm of true life and reality, in which all worth resides.
>
> In the course of the arguments that follow, it becomes still clearer that souls and Ideas are things of the same kind.[95]

---

94. Paul Friedländer, Plato, p. 64.

95. F.M. Cornford, From Religion to Philosophy, p. 246.

The focus and intent of Plato's work can be seen in terms of the method that Friedländer designates and the description of the relation between the soul and the realm of the forms or _Ideas_ given by Cornford. Plato, through myth, dialectic and the ecstasy of pure contemplation, pointed the ways which lead to ultimate knowledge. All of these ways or means pointed to the same goal. This goal included knowledge and cultivation of the rational aspect of the soul and an apprehension of the soul's relationship to the realm of _Ideas_, or ideal forms. The soul was of the same essential reality as the forms. It originated in the forms and would return to the forms. The soul found its true being in realizing its relationship to the forms.

From the analysis of the Socratic _daimon_, the phenomenon of divine madness, _ekstasis_, and the myth of the forms and the soul, a direct answer to the questions raised early in this chapter can be found. The major question raised by the position of Wilamowitz, Cornford, and Jaeger was this: If the philosophy of Plato and Socrates was a transformation of the religious tradition that proceeded, then was it not also possible that the reality symbolized by Dionysus was also integrated into their thought? In testing to see if the reality of Dionysus was retained, Plato and Socrates' apprehension of mystery, chaos, and unintelligibility was examined. The facets of Plato and Socrates' thought that seemed to be evidence for the apprehension of this phenomenon were found to be a dimension in which reason played the _dominant_ role. In the case of the _daimon_, it was found that the _daimon_ was the purest aspect of the rational part of the soul. In discussing the phenomenon of "divine madness," it was discerned that the ekstasis of this madness was not a result of being possessed by an irrational force, but from a depth experience of the realm of the forms. In this case the individual did not contact the dark, chaotic, mysterious, and irrational, but he caught a glimpse of ultimate intelligibility and clarity. In the myth of the forms the rational soul was the connection with this realm and even though this realm was often pointed to in terms of myths, it was a realm that supplied the ultimate basis for rational intelligibility. Thus, if Wilamowitz, Cornford, and Jaeger want to contend that Greek Philosophy was essentially part of the development of Greek religion, there should be no major quarrel with them if they recognize one significant qualification. This qualification is that in Socrates' and Plato's transformation of the Greek religious tradition, reason was the ultimate factor in _reforming_ this religious tradition. Reason plays the most significant role in each of the facets of Plato and Socrates' thought that have been reviewed and thus it does seem just to contend, with Nietzsche, that reason did rise to a position of tyranny in the philosophy of Socrates and Plato.

The other major question that we posed at the beginning of this chapter was this: Is it necessary to differentiate in the context of this problem between the thought of Socrates and Plato? Clearly, no; the tyranny that Socrates exhibited with his employment of the tightly rational and logical dialectic was also exhibited by Plato in his myth of the forms. In both cases reason plays a dominant or tyrannical role. In the dialectic it was the cutting edge that divided the true from the false. In the myth of the forms it was the capacity in man that could apprehend the truth through a penetration to the realm of the forms. Thus Socrates and Plato may have had different methods for pursuing truth, but both methods clearly reflect the tyranny of the rational.

Reflected in Socrates and Plato's tyranny of the rational and in the myth of the forms is an important assumption. This assumption is that reality is ultimately intelligible or there is an ultimate basis for knowledge. If man can cultivate this rational aspect of his soul he can comprehend the existence of this ultimate realm. Thus, the tyranny of the rational is necessary for Plato and Socrates, because for them only through subjugation and repression of darkness and mystery does light appear. This is in direct contrast to a crucial assumption of Nietzsche. For Nietzsche reality is essentially chaotic and mysterious. At best the intelligence can play with reality and seduce it into form but this form will be broken by the reemergence of chaos and mystery.[96] The interplay will once more begin between mystery and form and there will evolve a new synthesis. This process, that is, the interplay, must be maintained in order for creativity to occur. If form or intelligence banished mystery, thought will become abstract and out of touch with reality. If form does not seduce mystery into intelligibility, all will remain chaos. The individual recognizes that ultimate reality is "an essentially chaotic reality" and thus does not allow the tyranny of his reasoning to banish this chaos and mystery.

From this conflict of assumptions, it can be seen very clearly why Nietzsche would respond so vehemently to the tyranny exhibited by Socrates and Plato. Socrates and Plato, through their rational

---

96. Arthur C. Danto, Nietzsche as Philosopher (2nd ed.; New York, The MacMillan Co., 1968. London: Collier-MacMillan Limited, 1968), p. 30.

philosophies,banished the mystery that Nietzsche saw to be the very essence of reality. The tragic poet, according to Nietzsche, had played with this mystery and thus had achieved a level of awesome creativity. The rational tyranny of Socrates and Plato represented a definite decline in a culture which through its poets had once promoted the essence of creativity. Dionysus was banished; reason or the rational daimon was deified and Greek culture became "absurdly rational."

CHAPTER IV

BEYOND NIETZSCHE

"One repays a teacher badly if one always remains a pupil only."

Friedrich Nietzsche

In looking closely at the assumptions of Nietzsche and Socrates, there is a way in which the conflict between them can be utilized. Nietzsche maintained that reality at its base was essentially chaotic. Socrates, on the other hand, argued that reality (that is, the forms) provided the foundation for ultimate intelligibility. Clashing these assumptions together results in a dissonant contradiction; but holding them in tension can evoke a kind of harmony. There is, in other words, a way that reason can be used fruitfully, but not tyrannically. Holding in tension the possibilities that reality is ultimately chaotic and that reality is ultimately intelligible could provide the way of restraining reason from abusive tyranny.

The inquiry at hand would then be dialectically qualified by each of these assumptions. While proceeding to clarify a particular concept and to rationally bring it to intelligibility, a contrast to this method would be developed entertaining the possibility that reality is essentially mysterious and unintelligible. While enhancing the reality of mystery and chaos, it is possible to contrast this with the prospect that mystery could be made intelligible and behind the chaos there could be structure. In this dialectical movement of contrasts, reason would be employed as a tool for seeking clarity and apprehending structure. It would be stimulated by the possibility of ultimate knowledge and qualified by the possibility that reality, in its essence, is mysterious or chaotic. In rationally pursuing, for example, an understanding of a particular myth or poem, we would seek the meaning or structure that the myth or poem symbolically presented or represented. In this pursuit we would also accept the possibility that the myth or poem pointed to a mystery that we could not force into rational clarification. We would accept the poet's mode of knowing and expressing this knowledge as valid. We would not allow reason to become the tyrant that decided this validity.

In this way we would utilize the crucial assumptions of both Nietzsche and Plato. We would constantly hold open the possibility that at the base of reality there is form or structure and thus, be sensitive to Plato's myth or theory of the forms. In tension with this Nietzsche's assumption that, at base, reality is mysterious and unintelligible could be maintained. By this tension a descriptive definition of reason could be formed to hold reason in restraint. Reason would thus become a means of organizing reality or constructing a meaningful world. It would apprehend structure and form and it would recognize the existence of mystery. It would seek clarity and meaning but it would respect the meaning of meaninglessness.

This type of reason we would clearly distinguish from rationality. It would be a reason that is not restricted to logic or the rigors of argumentation. It would be a reason that viewed the syllogism and the fantasy or poem as equally valid and equally potent modes of expression. It would listen to the rationality of the argument but not identify itself with the rationality of the argument. Reason, given this orientation, would attempt to interpret the poet's insights or message. It would cooperate metaphorically with the reality pointed to by the poet. Reason thus would not capture the essence of the poem and force it into an argument which would be subject to tests of truth or falsity. Reason would search for the meaning of a poem and attempt to enhance this meaning by cooperation with the reality on which this meaning depends. Reason would not establish itself as the criterion for truth or falsity as is the case for the reason of rationality. Reason would be the organizing and responding agent of the intellect. It would function out of openness and find its strength in organizing, responding and apprehending. It would view itself as a responder or agent, not as a criterion or judge.

Through this redefinition of reason we would attempt a redefinition of the vocation of philosophy. What is being pointed to by means of this redefinition is the combination of the poet's vocation with the philosopher's vocation. In discussing Socrates and Plato's attitude toward the tragic poet, it was seen that Socrates and Plato wanted to banish the poet from the commonwealth which they had proposed, because the poet's works were penetrated with mystery and ambiguity. The poet's ability to pay attention to mystery and ambiguity can be combined with the philosopher's search for knowledge and intelligibility. The philosopher in searching for intelligibility should not allow his desire for clarity to banish mystery and ambiguity. He should find a way to pay attention to the mystery pointed to by the poet. If the philosopher viewed reason as an organizing, responding, and apprehending agent of the intellect, then it would seem that the philosopher could pay attention to the mystery pointed to by the poet. The philosopher would respond to the mystery which was named in the work of the poet and metaphorically cooperate with this mystery in order to enhance it and bring it to the apex of its expression.

Heidegger, in his response to the poetry of Hölderlin, serves as an example of the way a philosopher can respond with sensitivity and openness to the mystery named by the poet.

In the essay entitled "Remembrance of the Poet," Heidegger seeks to enhance and explicate the poem "Homecoming."[97] In this poem Hölderlin retraces his step metaphorically to the "source" of his being and Being. Hölderlin's return to his native soil and country is paralleled with Hölderlin's return to the mysterious source of his Being. Homecoming is the return to the proximity of the source, but it is also the realization that the sought-after source is not near. Although it is being approached, this source still remains distant. Coming to know the proximity of the source is a realization of mystery. Heidegger responds to this mystery in the following:

> But now if homecoming means becoming at home in proximity to the source, then must not the return home consist chiefly, and perhaps for a long time, in getting to know this mystery, or even first of all in learning how to get to know it. But we never got to know a mystery by unveiling or analyzing it; we only get to know it by carefully guarding the mystery <u>as</u> mystery. But how can it be carefully guarded--this mystery of proximity--without even being known? For the sake of this knowledge there must always be another who comes home for the first time and tells of the mystery.[98]

Heidegger describes the vocation of the poet as "homecoming" and as giving form to the experience of mystery which occurs at the proximity of the source.

> The vocation of the poet is homecoming, by which the homeland is first made ready as the land of proximity to the source. To guard the mystery of the reserving proximity to the Most Joyous, and in the process of guarding it to unfold it--that is the care of homecoming.[99]

---

97. Martin Heidegger, <u>Existence and Being</u>, with Intro. by Werner Brock (Chicago: Henry Regnery Company, 1949), pp. 233-269.

98. <u>Ibid</u>., p. 259.

99. <u>Ibid</u>., p. 266.

Heidegger suggests that one of the poet's most significant functions is to guard the "mystery of proximity." We do not get to know this mystery by unveiling or analyzing it, but we allow it to exist as mystery and guard the mystery in order for it to remain mystery. Taking his cue from the poet, Heidegger proceeds in his philosophical inquiry in much the same way. He does not banish mystery through a reductionistic analysis or through the tyranny of his rationality. He stands with the poet and allows the mystery to disclose itself as mystery. Heidegger through his openness and responsiveness exemplifies the type of reasoning that I am promoting and describing. He responds, apprehends and enhances the mystery to which the poet directs our attention. Thus Heidegger has been able to combine the vocation of the poet and the philosopher by paying attention to the mystery of the poet and cautiously restraining his search for intelligibility so that it would not banish the mystery pointed to by the poet.

Heidegger also exemplifies this posture of openness and responsiveness in his ability to combine the vocation of the philosopher and the poet in the dialogue entitled, "Conversation on a Country Path."[100] This dialogue consists of the conversation between a Teacher, a Scholar, and a Scientist. These individuals are reflecting on the nature of thinking. As the conversation evolves it occurs to them that they can "name" thinking but that they cannot rigorously define what they have named.

> Scientist: Then we can't really describe what we have named?
> Teacher: No. Any description would reify it.
> Scholar: Nevertheless it lets itself be named, and being named it can be thought about...
> Teacher: ...only if thinking is no longer re-presenting.
> Scientist: But then what else would it be?
> Teacher: Perhaps we now are close to being released into the nature of thinking...
> Scholar: ...through waiting for its nature.
> Teacher: Waiting, all right; but never awaiting, for awaiting already links itself with re-presenting and what is re-presented.
> Scholar: Waiting, however, lets go of that; or rather I should say that waiting lets re-presenting entirely alone. It really has no object.

---

100. Martin Heidegger, Discourse on Thinking, trans. by John M. Anderson and E. Hans Freund (New York: Harper & Row, Publishers, 1966), pp. 58-99.

Scientist: Yet if we wait we always wait for something.
Scholar: Certainly, but as soon as we re-present to our selves and fix upon that for which we wait, we really wait no longer.
Teacher: In waiting we leave open what we are waiting for.
Scholar: Why?
Teacher: Because waiting releases itself into openness...
Scholar: ...into the expanse of distance...
Teacher: ...in whose nearness it finds the abiding in which it remains.
Scientist: But remaining is a returning.
Scholar: Openness itself would be that for which we could do nothing but wait.
Scientist: But openness itself is that-which-regions...
Teacher: ...into which we are released by way of waiting, when we think.
Scientist: Then thinking would be coming-into-the-nearness of distance.[101]

Two of the key words of this passage are "openness" and "waiting." Heidegger finds it most appropriate to wait in openness and to be informed by the nature of thinking rather than trying to articulate a tightly formulated definition. This attitude seems to be completely non-aggressive because Heidegger appears to be more concerned with a passive posture of openness than with forcing the nature of thinking into intelligibility. However, this non-aggression might better be described as a responsiveness to the mystery of the nature of thinking. It is not completely passive because it responds to the mystery of the nature of thinking by naming it the "coming to the nearness of distance." Heidegger is not giving up his search for intelligibility but is balancing this search with the posture of openness and waiting. The type of balance that Heidegger displays in his search for intelligibility is very close to the balanced reason we have proposed early in this chapter. In our description reason retained its balance by holding in tension the possibility that reality is ultimately chaotic and that reality is ultimately intelligible. In this way we tried to be sensitive to the crucial assumptions of both Nietzsche and Socrates. Heidegger does not seem to operate with these assumptions, but he does display the kind of balanced relationship between mystery and intelligibility or, in other words, between the poet and the philosopher.

---

101. Ibid., pp. 67-68.

Reflecting upon Nietzsche's reaction to the tyranny of rationality in Socrates, our defense of this reaction, and our proposed re-definition of reason and the vocation of the philosopher, we find there is another reason for not ending our study in simple agreement with the insights of Nietzsche. First of all, Nietzsche in reacting against Socrates,could have also been reacting against the severely rationalistic philosophy of Hegel and his philosophical predecessors. In our own way we may have been involved in the same type of reactions. In our century we are not confronted by the towering speculative rationalism of Hegel, as was Nietzsche, but we are confronted by the harshly rational methods of analytic philosophy. It is possible that we are viewing Socrates in terms of our reaction to the way reason is employed and abused in our own times. Thus we must admit that our reaction to the abuse of reason and Nietzsche's understanding of Socrates is not a result of an a historical response to the thought of a philosopher who lived over two thousand years ago. A contemporary understanding of abusive rationality and our analysis of Socrates and Plato has been determined in part by the development of many centures of rational philosophy. Thus our proposed re-definition of reason and the vocation of philosophy was not only constructed in view of Socratic and Platonic reason but also in view of the abusive and tyrannical way in which reason is employed in our times.

ESSAY II:

AN INTERPRETATION OF NIETZSCHE'S PHILOSOPHY OF THE "WILL TO POWER"

The purpose of this essay is to construct an interpretation of Nietzsche's philosophy of the "will to power." This interpretation shall be developed in view of other major figures in late 18th and early 19th century philosophy. The present study will begin with Kant and the dimension of his philosophy that is the most relevant to understanding and interpreting the works of Nietzsche. An argument shall be elaborated that the emphasis upon the will, i.e., the volitional aspect of man, that is in the tradition of German philosophy extending from Kant to Nietzsche, stems out of, and arises in response to, Kant's ethics or moral philosophy. It will be demonstrated that the emphasis that Kant places upon the will and volition, developing and changing into a variety of forms and perspectives in the thought of Fichte, Schwelling and Schopenhauer, reaches its culmination in Nietzsche's "Wille zur Macht."

The essay at hand is not an attempt to reduce the problematics of these philosophers to Kant's questions and contentions. It is, however, an interpretative exercise in describing the interplay and interrelatedness of their ideas. A cause and effect sequence will not be found until the figures are discussed. All the philosophy in this tradition is not a mere chain reaction to Kant. This essay explains the "will to power" by examining the philosophical landscape out of which it grew. Kant will be the starting point, realizing that a more complete study would push much further back into the history of ideas.

In order to understand Kant's conception of the will, the inquirer must examine Kant's ethics. To interpret Kant's ethics, the significance that ethics had for Kant as a philosopher shall first of all be discussed. Thus, the initial question is this: Is ethics a central issue for Kant? Do ethics lie at the life center of his philosophy? The initial way of answering this question can be found through looking at Kant's career as a teacher.

In reviewing the courses that Kant offered during his teaching career, it can be seen that ethics was central to his work. From Kant's earliest years as a teacher he offered courses on ethics regularly. "From Arnold's list we know that he lectured regularly on ethics through all the years of his university life."[1]

---

1. Schilpp, Kant's Pre-Critical Ethics, p. 8. Schilpp is referring to the list constructed by E. Arnold which is a list of all the university courses offered by Kant. Cf. E. Arnold Kirtsche Exkurse im Gebiete der Kantforschumg.

Since Kant did offer courses on ethics on a regular basis, it would seem that he was genuinely concerned with ethics and regarded it as an area of importance. It is possible, however, that Kant could have lectured on ethics in order to show that ethics was a frivolous and insignificant endeavor. A brief look at the lecture notes assembled by Kant's students will suffice to rule this out as a possibility. In the Lectures on Ethics it is clearly evident that Kant did not merely deal with ethics in order to expose it as an insignificant matter. Kant lectured on ethics as part of his attempt to establish a "Universal Practical Philosophy." Ethics was Kant's practical philosophy. He sought to establish ethics as a science or as a systematic discipline. He sought to establish a discipline that has for its object of concern, practice.

> ...practical philosophy is practical not in respect of its form, but of its object. It is a theory of practice. Just as logic is a science of reason, not in respect of its form but because its object is the mind, so ethics must have a practical object, i.e., practice.[2]

Kant is thus clearly concerned with establishing an ethic. It can be deduced from his concern for ethics as a teacher that ethics was central or at least significant to the life center of his philosophy.

Schilpp, in Kant's Pre-Critical Ethics, also offers evidence which aids the reader in validating the contention that ethics was a major concern in Kant's philosophy. Commenting specifically on Kant's early writings, Schilpp has this to say:

> There are many other proofs of Kant's early interest in problems or morality. In the first place, several of his earlier writings show, either directly or indirectly, a concern with moral issues. Among these are: Algemeine Naturgeschichte und Theorie des Himmels (1757); Entwurf und Ankundigung eines Collegii der Physischen Geographie (1757); Versuch einiger Betrachtungen uber den Optimismus (1759); Versuch den Begriff der negativen Grossen in die Weltweisheit einzufuhren (1763); Untersuchung uber die Duetlichkeit der Grundastze der naturlichen Theologie und der Moral (1764); Beobachtungen uber das Gefuhl des Schonen und Erhabenen (1764); the already quoted Nachricht von der

---

2. Kant, Immanuel, Lectures on Ethics. Trans. by Louis Infield, (New York and Evanston: Harper Torchbooks, 1963), p. 3.

Einrichtung seiner Vorlesungen in dem Winterhalbenjahre von (1765-1766); Traume eines Geistershers (1766); his inaugural dissertation at the occasion of the beginning of his full professorship of logic and metaphysics at the University of Konigsberg, De Mundi sensibilis atque intelligibilis forma et principiis (1770); and finally a certain Fragment which appears to date from 1763, 1764 or 1765.[3]

Since Kant did not devote an entire work to systematically analyzing ethics as a philosophical possibility until after he wrote his first major critique, the Critique of Pure Reason, it has been often popularly contended that ethics was a side issue that arose after the Critique of Pure Reason. Schilpp offers an explanation that renders this contention invalid. According to Schilpp, Kant did not systematically develop his ethics until after he analyzed epistemology and metaphysics because Kant realized that epistemology and ethics were deeply interrelated.

> It is equally clear that, whatever may have been his interest in ethics before 1785, Kant never permitted himself to write in detail on ethical problems until he had cleared the ground for his ethical work by giving his answer to the problems of metaphysics and especially to those of epistemology. He realized that until he had determined what was the nature of knowledge and what it was possible for man to know, it was useless to try to answer questions requiring ethical knowledge.[4]

In order to understand Kant's ethics, a look to the epistemological problems that surround his ethics is necessary. Kant begins his inquiry into the nature of ethics and moral judgements in the following way. He begins with the "fact" of morality. Kant contends that it is clear from our experience that there is a phenomena which we call morality, i.e., we see and experience human beings making moral judgements. The question then for Kant is not whether morality in fact exists but what is the basis for moral judgements. The movement of Kant's questioning concerning the validity of moral judgements is parallel to his inquiry into the basis of science. Kant has in the foreground of his concern Newtonian physics when he makes this inquiry. He accepts Newtonian physics as valid. He thinks that Newton has correctly

---

3. Schilpp, Paul, Kant's Pre-Critical Ethics, (Evanston and Chicago: Northwestern University: 1938, p. 9).

4. Schilpp, Kant's Pre Critical Ethics, p. 10.

understood the relationships between objects in nature. Kant's inquiry does not question or challenge the validity of Newton's discoveries; Kant is solely concerned with explaining how a science of nature is possible. Kant is also concerned with seeking out the epistemological basis for ethics. Thus, in both cases, in ethics and natural science Kant begins with a fact. In the case of ethics he begins with the fact of morality; in science, he begins with the "fact" that Newton's physics is valid. In each case he is seeking out the method and the epistemological basis for the knowledge that gives us science and that produces ethical judgements. Each of these disciplines has its proper object, according to Kant. Science has for its object the world of appearance, the world of phenomenon. Ethics has for its object the moral activity of man.

There is a radical difference between the two realms known to science and morality respectively. The radical difference is exemplified in the fact that for Kant the world of nature is strictly determined and that the world of ethics is free. Kant defines nature in the following way and in this definition, it is clear that he understands nature to be determined. "Nature is the existence of things so far as it is determined according to universal laws."[5] What does Kant mean by determined? Are things in themselves determined? What is humankind's relationship to this rigidly determined nature? According to Kant, the knower does the determining, that is, we organize and determine the realm of nature with our intellect. How does this determination occur? In the world of appearance we perceive change. In response to this change, we organize the relationships between the objects involved in this change in terms of cause and effect. According to Kant, this organization in terms of cause and effect occurs universally. When we see an object in motion, we immediately conclude that something caused this motion. As a result, we organize all appearances around the principle of cause and effect, that is, we determine all objects in the phenomenal world by our organizing them as causes and effects. "All alterations take place in conformity with the law of the connection of cause and effect."[6] The determination and lack of freedom that Kant

---

5. Kant, Immanuel. Prolegomena To Any Future Metaphysics, (New York: The Bobbs-Merrill Company, Inc., 1950), p. 42.

6. Kant, Immanuel, Critique of Pure Reason, (New York: St. Martin's Press, 1965), p. 218.

assigns to the realm of nature can be seen in yet another way. Cause and effect in this case become the basis for the possibility of scientific knowledge. When we contend that heat causes metal objects to expand we are, according to Kant, making a universal statement. We are stating a universal law of nature. Heat must expand metal in all cases and the metal must not have any choice in this matter. It must occur universally. If the metal could arbitrarily choose whether it wanted to expand, scientific statements would be meaningless. They would be meaningless because they would only be a projection of what might occur. Science, according to Kant, is knowledge which is universally valid. It is not projection of guessing. The source of universality and necessity can be discerned in the following example.

> As an easier example, we may take the following: "When the sun shines on the stone, it grows warm." This judgement, however often I and others may have perceived it, is a mere judgement of perception and contains no necessity; perceptions are only usually conjoined in this manner. But if I say, "The sun warms the stone," I add to the perception a concept of the understanding, namely, that of cause, which necessarily connects with the concept of sunshine that of heat, and the synthetical judgement becomes of necessity universally valid, namely objective, and is converted from a perception into experience.[7]

Thus, the intellect adds universal necessity by associating causes with effects. Since all of us organize sensation in terms of cause and effect, we all experience the same relationships in nature. On the basis of the similarity of the organizing activity of our intellects we can have knowledge that is universally valid for all mankind.

In shifting our attention to ethics,the reader can see that Kant is also seeking universal laws that regulate activity in this realm. As was stated previously, the fact from which Kant makes his departure is the fact of morality. Kant says it is self-evident that morality exists and he is not challenging its existence. He accepts its existence and is merely trying to philosophically determine how it is possible, that is, he attempts to discern what is the basis for moral judgements. Moving from the fact of morality Kant asks what conditions are necessary for morality to occur. Freedom appears to be the primary condition that gives rise to the possibility of morality. "Freedom,

---

7. Kant, Prolegomena, p. 49.

however, among all the ideas of speculative reason is the only one whose possibility we know a priori. We do not understand it, but we know it as the condition of the moral law which we do know."[8] What does Kant mean by referring to freedom as a condition for morality? Kant argues that in order for morality to occur, human beings must be able to choose his/her course of action. Why must this be the case? In morality responsibility is essential, that is, when a person performs an action that is moral we hold him "morally" responsible for this action. If we hold individuals responsible for actions, then these actions must truly be their own. If an individual is to be held responsible for certain deeds, then he/she must be free to be the cause of these deeds. If a person possesses no freedom in his/her actions, he/she cannot be held responsible for these actions. If an individual is caught in a nexus of cause and effect which he/she cannot intercept and become a cause of his/her actions, then he/she cannot be held responsible for these actions.

Up until this point, Kant has moved from the fact of morality and deduced from this fact that an individual must be free, if the making of moral decisions is to be taken seriously. Kant does not stop at this point, but goes on to expose principles that regulated moral activity. Through the function of practical reason, Kant arrives at principles that regulate and organize moral decisions. Kant is seeking at this juncture a moral law that will be universally valid. Why is universal validity so important for Kant? Kant contends that unless a moral principle is universally valid, it is meaningless. If a principle that regulates moral action is only true for some cases, then, in fact, it is not a principle at all. It is merely a guess or at best a conjecture. In ethics, like science, Kant is seeking universal laws that hold true in all cases. Kant finds this principle in the moral or categorical imperative which he describes as the "Fundamental Law of Pure Practical Reason." It takes the form of the following: "So act that the maxim of your will could always hold at the same time as a principle establishing universal law."[9] Practical reason directs the activity of the will through this regulating principle.

The importance that Kant ascribes to the functioning of the will and the activity of practical reason cannot be underestimated. The functions of the will for Kant are the apex of human activity. Humankind is truly fulfilling their potential when they exercise their personal will and activate practical reason. Kant's deep admiration for the human will is exemplified when he discusses the

---

9. Kant, Critique of Practical, p. 30.

good and what it is. Kant describes the significance of the will in this way: "nothing in the world, indeed nothing even beyond the world, can possibly be conceived which could be called good without qualification except a good will."[10] The will, thus, is the most noble aspect of human nature. Kant sets the action of the will above all other human functions. Moral knowledge becomes the most significant knowledge. Practical reason thus is seen to be superior to theoretical reason. Kroner describes Kant's preference for the practical reason as the "primacy of practical reason." Kroner contends that the will is the focal point of Kant's philosophy or that "the will is the focal point of Kant's Weltanschauung."[11] Why is it the focal point; why is the will the apex of human consciousness? The will connects man with the noumenal realm. The will lifts the self beyond appearance. The will connects human beings with ultimate reality. Kroner describes this as the metaphysical significance of moral activity:

> What renders moral activity metaphysically significant is precisely Kant's conviction that the supersensible speaks through morality; it is Kant's contention that the moral realm points to the ultimate ground of all being and all existence.[12]

---

10. Kant, Critique of Practical Reason, p. 55.

11. Kroner, Richard, Kant's Weltanschauung, (Chicago: University of Chicago Press, 1956), pp. 6-7.

12. *Ibid.*, p. 31.

The will lifts man beyond the realm of nature, beyond the realm of phenomena.[13]

Growing out of Kant's deification of the will and his assignment of priority to practical reason there emerges a radical separation between humankind and nature. Persons, according to Kant, become fully human when they separate themselves from nature. When a self lifts itself above the causal nexus and chooses, it realizes its freedom and becomes fully human. Human nature consists of two egos, an empirical ego and a pure ego. The empirical ego is the ego that functions according to scientific laws. The pure ego is the "I" which goes beyond scientific laws. The empirical ego "I" knows and responds to objects in the phenomenal world, the world of appearance whereas the pure ego links the self with the noumenal world.

---

13. An emphasis upon will and moral decision is also a prevalent theme in German literary sources in the Kantian era. In Schiller's Wallenstein, for example, we see that moral behaviour is a crucial determinant in the success and failure of Wallenstein. When Wallenstein acts with moral consistency he succeeds and is able to read his course of action in the stars. When he betrays his superiors he breaks the moral harmony he participated in and falls into ruin and defeat. Another example that suggests a simiar theme concerning the nobility and importance of the "good moral will" is Goethe's Iphigenie auf Tauris. Iphigenie triumphs and is able to win her freedom from King Thoas because she does not betray him and flee against his will. Her moral integrity impresses the king greatly and she wins her freedom because she chose loyalty over deceit. Again in this work, the good moral will is the key to the human situation and it is the apex of human activity. Goethe and Schiller differ slightly with Kant in that nature seems to affirm and support moral activity in Goethe and Schiller's view,but nature is something man must rise above and from which he must separate himself for moral decision in the perspective of Kant. Man transcends the natural world in moral activity according to Kant but for Goethe and Schiller, at least as it is presented in the above works, man participates deeply in the moral harmony of nature and the universe when he acts morally. (See Goethe Iphigenie auf Tauris, ed. by L.A. Thoader, D.C. Heath and Co., Boston 1961 and Schiller's Wallensteins Tod, ed. by William Witte and Basil Blackwell, 1966).

Kant attempts to heal this radical bifurcation in his Aesthetics. In Kant's third critique, the Critique of Judgement, he "seeks to throw a bridge across the deep moat separating nature and morality, determinism and freedom, the sensible and intelligible world."[14] In the experience of beauty, human consciousness views a mechanistic and determined nature in a decisively different way. According to Kant, the aesthetic judgement responding to the experience of beauty brings humankind into a close relationship with determined nature. How does this occur? Through the aesthetic judgement we come to know a mechanistically determined nature as purposeful.[15] Momentarily in the confrontation with a work of art or a beautiful landscape, humankind experiences itself organically as a part of purposeful nature. The aesthetic experience and the judgement issuing from it only temporarily reconcile the realms known to science and ethics. The harmony between these two realms is only viewed momentarily.

Fichte continues the Kantian emphasis on the prominence of the will and moral action. Fichte develops a philosophy of Tathandlung, a philosophy that centers around deeds and activity. Marias, in tracing the development of Fichte's philosophy, describes Fichte's relationship to Kant in the following way:

> Fichte's philosophy is directly derived from Kant's. At the beginning, he presents his philosophy as a mature and profound exposition of Kantianism. But it is difficult to see this philosophical genesis if we adhere to the popular image of Kant handed down to us by the nineteenth century. It is necessary to return to the point at which Kant summed up the meaning of his philosophy.
>
> The culmination of Kantian philosophy was practical reason. Kant ended by affirming the primacy of practical over theoretic reason, and the moral person, Kant's pure ego, determined himself practically and unconditionally. The self-determination of the ego by practical

---

14. Collins, James. A History of Modern European Philosophy, Milwaukee: The Bruce Publishing Company, 1954.

15. Kant, The Critique of Judgement, pp. 132ff.

> reason is very clearly seen in the form that could be given to the categorical imperative: do what you will, emphasizing the will; do what you are able to will. For Fichte, the moral imperative consists of saying: become the man you are (werde, der du bist), and in this sense Fichte's imperative is not far removed from Kant's, because when Kant says, "Do what you will" or Be free," he asks man to act in accordance with what he ultimately is, to determine himself, with freedom. In this way the empirical ego, which is determined by many things, ought to act, according to Kant, as if it were free, or, expressed differently, the empirical ego ought to aim to be the pure ego that it is essentially. Thus Fichte tells man: "Be the man you are," aim to be the man you are essentially. In Fichte (as in Kant, when all is summed up) morality consists in adjusting to what one truly is, in not falsifying oneself.[16]

Thus, for both Kant and Fichte, becoming fully human can be accomplished through the exercising of the moral will. A person, determining himself/herself in moral and responsible action, rises from the level of a determined object to genuine selfhood. A person becomes truly human by exercising and developing the volitional capacity or dimension. Fichte poetically spells out this position in his work called The Vocation of Man. He searches first of all through the intricate labyrinth of doubt and then moves to explore humankinds' relation to nature. His question is "What am I myself, and what is my vocation?" He finds no answer that satiates the thirst of his question through viewing a person as nature so he moves expectantly to exploring the possibility of self as Spirit. The dimensions and dynamics of self as spirit are also subtle, intricate, and profound but Fichte does not find the essence of human beings to be spirit. Fichte turns then to the will and action as a solution. He asks again and answers his initial question in the following manner:

> And what, then, is this something lying beyond all presentation, towards which I stretch forward with such ardent longing? What is the power with which it draws me towards it? What is the central point in my soul to which it is attached, and with which only it can be effaced?

---

16. Marias, Julian. History of Philosophy, pp. 308-9.

"Not merely TO KNOW, but according to thy knowledge TO DO, is thy vocation:--thus is it loudly proclaimed in the innermost depths of my soul, as soon as I recollect myself for a moment, and turn my observation upon myself. Not for idle contemplation of thyself, not for brooding over devout sensations;--no, for action art thou here; thine action, and thine action alone, determines thy worth."[17]

Fichte, like Kant, contends that humankind reaches the fulfillment of its nature in moral activity. Self activity, not self reflection, is the goal of humanity. Contemplation and "idle brooding" are trivialities--man's vocation is "to do."[18]

---

17. Fichte, Johann Gottlieb, The Vocation of Man, pp. 93-94.

18. The primacy and priority of will and action is also an important theme in Goethe's Faust. Faust shortly before his first encounter with Mephistopheles gives action decisive priority:

'Tis written, "In the beginning was the Word." Here I am balked! Who, now, can help afford? The Word-- impossible so high to rate it; quite otherwise must I translate it, if by the Spirit's light I'm truly taught. I've writ, "In the beginning was the Thought." This first line let me weigh completely, lest my impatient pen proceed too fleetly. Is it the Mind which works, creates, indeed? "In the beginning was the Power,"now I read. Yet, as I write, a warning is suggested, that I the sense may not have fairly tested. The Spirit aids me, now I see the light! "In the beginning was the Act." I write.

Geschrieben steht: "Im Anfang war das Wort!" Hier stock' ich schon! Wer hilft mir weiter fort? Ich kann das Wort so hoch unmoglich schatzen, ich muss es anders ubersetzen, wennich vom Gieste recht erleuchtet bin. Geschrieben steht: Im Anfang war der Sinn. Bedenke wohl die erste Zeile, dass deine Feder sich nicht ubereile! Ist es der Sinn, der alles wirkt und schafft? Es sollte stehn: Im anfang war die Kraft! Doch, auch indem ich dieses niederschreibe, schon warnt mich was, dass ich dabei nicht bleibe. Mir hilft der Geist? auf einmal seh'ich Bat und schreibe getrost: Im Anfang war die Tat!

von Goethe, J.W. Faust, trans. by Bayard Taylor, New York: Collier Books, 1962, pp. 114-15.

The will differentiates humankind from nature because the will elevates the self beyond the sensual and natural world into the realm of freedom and pure spirit. The will gives a person a distinctive identify. Fichte describes the distinctiveness of the will in the following way:

> My will is mine, and it is the only thing that is wholly mine and entirely dependent on myself; and through it I have already become a citizen of the realm of freedom and of pure spiritual activity.[19]

For Fichte, as for Kant, the will is the mark of distinctiveness in man. The will separates man from mere nature. Man is uniquely free, that is, he exercises the freedom of self-determination.

In Schelling's Naturphilosophie, the reader confronts an intriguing reformation of the problem of freedom, nature and will. In the early phases of Schelling's philosophy, one finds him to be closely related to the problematics of Fichte's philosophy,but in the later works,especially in Philosophische Untersuchen uber das Wesen der menschlichen Freiheit und die damit Zusammenhangenden Gegenstande,we see a unique and decisively distinct position emerging. Schelling, dissatisfied with Kant's view of nature, that is, viewing nature as determined and in no respect free, develops a position that challenges the Kantian dichotomy between human kind and nature. Schelling disagrees with Kant and Fichte and claims he would deny the existence of freedom before he would contend that only the ego has will and freedom.

> Kurzer oder entscheidender are, das System auch im Wille oder Verstande des Urwesens zu leugnen; zu sagen, dass es uberhaupt nur einzelne Willen gebe, deren jeder einen Mittelpunkt fur sich ausmache, und nach Fichte's Ausdruck eines jeden Ich die Absolut Substanz sei.[20]

The locus of freedom and will is shifted and broadened. For Schelling, the ego or the self is merely one expression of the over-arching will and freedom of the Absolute. There is no radical

---

19. Fichte. Vocation, pp. 134-5.

20. Schelling Werke, Vol. I, part VII, p. 337.

discontinuity between man and nature. Nature is seen as a dynamic and creative process, freely unfolding and human nature is a vital part of this evolution. In human consciousness, nature can recollect itself or remember itself in its previous forms.[21]

> "Die platonische Idee, dass alle Philosophie Erinnerung sei, ist in diesem Sinne wahr: alles Philosophiren besteht in einen Erinnern des Zustandes, in welchem wir eins waren mit der Nature."[22]

Schelling does not view nature as a mass of causal sequences or determined patterns. Nature is a unity of creativity and becoming, not a unity of mechanical laws. Schelling contends that nature has an "inner union" and a "living reason."[23] Schelling accuses Fichte of being a "mere mechanist" and also that Fichte sees nature merely as an arena for human purposes and action.[24] Schelling seeks to go beyond the human preoccupation with self and freedom and articulates the living continuity of humanity and nature, a unity that Schelling experiences mystically and ecstatically.[25] The all-pervasive unity of Being is a unity of will

---

21. In A. Alexander's Theories of the Will in the History of Philosophy, page 291, we find the intelligence and dynamism of nature described in the following way: "Nature according to Schelling is not dead but only unconscious. It is not being but becoming. It is a process the end of which is intelligence."

22. Schelling, Werke, Vol. I, part IV, p. 77.

23. Schelling, Werke, Vol. I, part VIII, Ueber das Wesen Deutscher Wissenschaft (aus dem handschriftlichen Nachlass).

24. Schelling, Werke, Vol. I, part VII, p. 103. Darlegung des Verhaltnisses der Naturphilosophie zu der verbesserten Fichteschen Lehre.

25. In Bolman's introduction to The Ages of the World, p. 48, we find the following description of Schelling's mystical apprehensions:

> "Put it another way, he was reapplying Bohme's mystic primal reality (or ungrounded) and ground it in a context where, first, a science will be the highest science in accounting for finite existence. In brief, he was trying to translate Bohme's vision into a science which included freedom."

according to Schelling. The will is something more than the apex of human activity: it is the form that all of being assumes. Schelling states this contention as follows: "Es gibt in der lezten un hochsten Instanz gar kein anderes Sein als Wollen... Wollen ist Ursein..."[26] The will is being, therefore to will is to participate in the essence of reality. The will is the primordial essence of nature and also of human nature. Schelling's "Naturphilosophie" thus includes human beings because humanity and nature are linked in the unity of will. "Will, therefore, is the eternal principle of the Universe" in the philosophy of Schelling.[27]

The pervasive reality of will is also a key issue in the philosophy of Schopenhauer. For Schopenhauer there are two facets or levels to reality and both of these dimensions can be known. Schopenhauer constructs his philosophy in view of the Kantian distinction between the phenomenal and noumenal realms. For Kant, our knowledge of things is limited to the phenomenal realm, that is, we can know things insofar as they are phenomena or insofar as they appear to us. We cannot know things or objects as they are in themselves. Schopenhauer, like Kant, contends that the basis for knowledge or the root of knowledge is the knowing subject. "That which knows all things and is known by none is the subject. It is accordingly the supporter of the world, the universal condition of all that appears, of all objects and it is always pre-supposed; for whatever exists, exists only for the subject."[28] This grounding of knowledge in the knowing subject is present in the philosophy of Schopenhauer from his very early writings. In his doctoral dissertation, On the Fourfold Root of Sufficient Reason, Schopenhauer contends that every object insofar as it is known is conditioned by subjective principles. Every object of knowledge is an "object for a subject." Schopenhauer does not contend, however, that everything that is to become an object of knowledge for us must have a sufficient reason.[29]

---

26. Schelling, Sammtliche Werke, Vol. I, part VII, p. 350.

27. Alexander, Theories of the Will, p. 308.

28. Schopenhauer, The World as Will and Idea, Vol. I, p. 5.

29. Collins, James. The History of Modern European Philosophy, p. 665.

Reason, thus, is a regulative and formalizing function in the philosophy of Schopenhauer. Reason does not apprehend the rationality of the object in itself but it conditions the object sufficiently so that it can be known. It organizes sensations according to principles and regulates them into forms of intelligibility. Schopenhauer describes the a priori conditioning and conditions of experience in the following way:

> All our presentations stand toward one another in a regulated connection, which may be determined a priori, and on account of which, nothing existing separately and independently, nothing single or detached, can become an object for us. It is this connection which is expressed by the principle of Sufficient Reason in its generality.[30]

Thus, on the basis of the a priori principles and conditioning of the knowing subject, knowledge is attained and determined. This is the world of Vorstellung, or the world as idea and representation. It is the world as idea in the mind of the knower; the world as represented and determined.

For Schopenhauer there is a realm beyond the realm of appearance that also can be known. This is the realm of the primordially relentless and eternal will. Reason, order, necessity, and determination belong to the world of appearance; will, freedom, and driving dynamism belong to the realm beyond appearance. As a result, every being in the world

> ...is on the one hand phenomenon and is necessarily determined by the laws of the phenomenon, it is on the other in itself will, indeed absolutely free will. For all necessity arises only through the forms that belong entirely to the phenomenon, namely the principle of sufficient reason in its different aspects. But then aseity must also belong to such a will, for as free, in other words,as thing-in-itself and thus not subordinate to the principle of sufficient reason.[31]

---

30. Schopenhauer. On the Fourfold Root of the Principle of Sufficient Reason, Part III, p. 16.

31. Schopenhauer. The World as Will and Representation, p. 320.

Reason thus is the determining agent in the realm of appearance, for it orders objects into forms of intelligibility. Will is the essence of the realm beyond appearance, the realm and reality that operates behind all that comes to us as representation. The will or the realm beyond appearance is the realm of the "Thing-in-Itself."[32] The genius of Schopenhauer resides in this contention, because in it Schopenhauer takes the Kantian distinction between phenomena and noumena, sets it alongside Kant's position on the priority of the willing subjects, and then drives these contentions to their logical conclusion. Kant, on the one hand, contended that "Things as they are in themselves" are unknowable, but yet on the other hand seems to imply that willing lifts man beyond appearance to the noumenal realm. Schopenhauer contends that if the transcendental ego (Kant's name for the moral will) becomes noumenal through willing and freedom, then the realm of the "Thing-in-Itself" must also be will and freedom. This contention also has continuity with the philosophy of Schelling, in that human nature is not an isolated island of volition, as is the case for Kant (so far as we can know this realm) but, as Schelling contends, will pervades all of nature or all that is. Schopenhauer took great care to examine aspects of nature and as a result went to great lengths to find evidence for his theories in biology. He finds the will operative

> not only [in] the voluntary actions of animals, but the organic mechanism, nay even the shape and quality of their living body, the vegetation of plants and finally, even in inorganic nature, crystalization, and in general every primary force which manifests itself in physical and chemical phenomena, not excepting gravity.[33]

---

32. Ibid. See Chapter XXV, "Transcendent Considerations of the Will as Thing-in-Itself."

33. Schopenhauer. On the Will in Nature, p. 217.

Will, for Schopenhauer, is not merely a function related to intelligence and rational beings; it is the key to all of being.[34] We confront an explicit example of this contention in a chapter in the second volume of his *magnum opus*, a chapter entitled, "On the Objectification of the Will in Nature without Knowledge." The contention is as follows:

> The first step in the fundamental knowledge of my metaphysics is that the will we find within us does not, as philosophy previously assumed, proceed first of all from knowledge; that it is not, in fact, a mere modification of knowledge, and thus something secondary, derived, and like knowledge itself, conditioned by the brain; but that it is the prius of knowledge, the kernel of our true being. The will is that primary and original force itself, which forms and maintains the animal body, in that it carries out that body's unconscious as well as conscious functions.[35]

But how can Schopenhauer validate such a contention? How do we know the world as will? Are we not limited to a knowledge of world as idea or representation? According to Schopenhauer, "Man carries the ultimate fundamental secrets within himself, and this

---

34. An interesting supplement occurs just before Schopenhauer's chapter on the *Thing in Itself*, pg. 189, Vol. II of *The World as Will and Idea.* The following quotation of Goethe is presented. It also exemplifies Schopenhauer's position concerning the unity of man and nature.

"Ihr folget falscher Spur
Denkt nicht, wir scherzen!
Ist nicht der Kern der Natur
Menschen im Herzen? (Goethe)

(You follow a false trail,
Think not that we jest!
Is not the core of nature
In the heart of men?" (Tr.)

35. Schopenhauer. *The World as Will and Idea*. Vol. II, p. 293.

fact is accessible to him in the most immediate way. Here only, therefore, can be the hope to find the key to the riddle of the world, and obtain a clue to the nature of all things."[36] This is the "very special providence of Metaphysics." It is humankind's "way in" to a knowledge of ultimate being or will. How does one decipher the ultimate nature of things? The self participates in this ultimate reality and as a result is his/her own key to it. Human self-consciousness comes to know itself as willing. This can be known immediately; it is present in the immediacy of reflective being. This immediacy brings humankind beyond self-knowledge and beyond an awareness of one's own being. It begins in immediacy but then moves by analogy from immediacy to all of being.

> Everyone knows only one being quite immediately, namely his own will in self-consciousness. He knows everything else only mediately, and then judges it by analogy with that one being; according to the degree of his power of reflection, this analogy is carried further. Even this springs ultimately and fundamentally from the fact that there is really only one being; the illusion of plurality (Maya), resulting from the forms of external, objective apprehension, could not penetrate right into the inner, simple consciousness; hence this always meets with only one being.[37]

Humankind, thus, knows the ultimate and pervasive will through the self and its willing. The self participates in the primordial unity of willing or the volitional unity of Being. The individual will, as a result, becomes a paradigm for the metaphysical will -- it is a moment of it because of its participation in it. Schopenhauer, however, does not promote or suggest that we truly know what we are by contemplating our individual will. To become overly enamoured with the will as our will or the will as our ego precludes us from intuiting and apprehending the basic oneness of all will. Schopenhauer suggests that we must go beyond the ego and beyond individuality for two basic and interrelated reasons. Going beyond the ego or individuality brings us to oneness of being and also the possibility of genuine moral activity. The oneness of Being and genuine moral activity are crucially and decisively interconnected in Schopenhauer's philosophy.

---

36. Ibid., p. 179.

37. Ibid., p. 321.

In describing the oneness of Being and Will, Schopenhauer makes consistent reference to the Vedas and Puranas. The world of appearance or the world of things Schopenhauer compares to the world of Maya. It is a world we take to be real but actually, as is the case in Vedic literature, the world of things and appearance is a "veil of deception which covers the eyes of mortals." Appearance attaches the mind to particulars, to things, or to objects. Reality, however, is not grasped by apprehending particulars; it is known only by penetrating beyond things and illusion and intuiting the eternal unity of Will.

This contention concerning the unity of all being becomes particularly important for Schopenhauer's book on a metaphysics of ethics, On the Basis of Morality. The chief and most significant anti-moral incentive according to Schopenhauer is "egoism." It is the primary motive activating human action and, as a result, the key of immorality.

> The chief and fundamental incentive in man as in the animal is egoism, that is, the craving for existence and well-being. The German word Selbstsucht (passion for self) involves a false secondary notion of disease. The word Eigennutz (self interest), however, denotes egoism insofar as this is under the guidance of the faculty of reason; by means of reflection, this faculty enables egoism to pursue its purposes systematically.[38]

The egoist, like the naive realist, is locked in the realm of individuality and particularity. He/she only regards his/her own individuality as real and significant. One is unable to go beyond one's own motives and interests and apprehend the continuity that the self has with others. In ethics like metaphysics, the ego must be abolished, individuality transcended, and the boundaries of self overcome. When the self is overcome, a person can identify with other human beings and rejoice and suffer in the unity of mankind. Ethical empathy and concern only come when

> I have identified myself with the other man, and in consequence the barrier between the ego and non-ego is for the moment abolished; only then do the other man's affairs, his need, distress, and suffering, directly become my own. I no longer look at him as if he were something given to me by empirical intuitive perception,

---

38. Schopenhauer. On the Basis of Morality, p. 131.

> as something strange and foreign, as a matter of indifference, as something entirely different from me. On the contrary, I share the suffering in him, in spite of the fact that his skin does not enclose my nerves. Only in this way can his woe, his distress, become a motive for me; otherwise it can be absolutely only my own.[39]

In the eyes of the immoral individual desires and motives are most real and supremely significant. In the eyes of the morally liberated person, an other's suffering is truly one's own. Walter Kaufmann contends that Schopenhauer "stressed the universality of suffering more than any previous philosopher."[40] This appears to be a valid contention because the major works of Schopenhauer are preoccupied with the analysis, description and ultimate release from human suffering.

Thus the key to metaphysical and ethical insight is compassion and the universalization of both being and suffering. Particulars, things, individuals and ego-oriented "separateness belongs to the realm of phenomenon."[41] True being and genuine compassion only arises when I apprehend the following:

> Individuation is mere phenomenon or appearance and originates through space and time. These are nothing but the forms of all of the objects of my cerebral cognitive faculty and are conditioned by them. And so even plurality and diversity of individuals are mere phenomenon, that is, exist only in my representation. My true inner being exists in every living thing as directly as it makes itself known in my self-consciousness only to me. In Sanskrit tat tvam asi (this art thou) is the formula, the standing expression, for this knowledge. It is this that bursts forth as compassion on which all genuine, i.e., disinterested, virtue therefore depends, and whose real expression is every good deed.[42]

When I apprehend and compassionately realize that "I am not I but I am thou and I am all" then the suffering of mankind truly becomes my own and my compassion responds to it and in it. True

---

39. Ibid. p. 166

40. Kaufmann, Walter. Tragedy and Philosophy, p. 339.

41. Schopenhauer. On the Basis, p. 209.

42. Ibid.

perception and insight occur when the individual apprehends and participates in the unity of all things.[43] The question now becomes: how can this realm be transcended or how can a human being be relieved of suffering if this driving volitional dynamism is at the core of Being? How can one escape this ruthless and tragic will?[44] By denying the personal will to live through the release of aesthetic indifference. Reacting against the will and opposing it ensnares the individual once again in the convulsion of action and volition. Reaction is an affirmative of the dominating power of will, whereas indifference and denial are a means of escaping this titanic dynamism. Man's tragic error lies in his "affirmative of the will to live; on the other hand, the denial of this will in consequence of the dawning of better knowledge is salvation."[45] Action and reaction still represent a clinging to will; aesthetic indifference and denial are the key to releasement and peace. Individuality is retained in reaction.

> But individuality is also inherent in the will, in so far as the character is individual; yet this character itself is abolished in the denial of the will. Thus, individuality is inherent in the will only in its affirmation, not in its denial.[46]

Superficially, it would seem that Schopenhauer is advocating suicide as salvation but, if the reader looks closer, it can be seen that this is definitely not the case. Individual death does not affect the ultimate functioning of will nor does it escape

---

43. On the closing page of On the Basis of Morality, p. 214, Schopenhauer quotes a passage from the Bhagavad-Gita. It, too, points to his contention concerning the oneness of all being. "He who sees the Supreme Lord abiding equally in all beings, never perishing when they perish, he, verily, sees."

44. In Thomas Mann's Essays of Three Decades, pp. 372-410, we find a most poetic and insightful description of Schopenhauer's understanding of will. Mann describes Schopenhauer's goal as an attempt to free men who are "trapped in the principium individuationis and shrouded in the veil of Maya." (p. 389).

45. Schopenhauer. The World as Will and Representation, Vol. II, p. 608.

46. Ibid. p. 609.

will. It is the last burst of ultimate volition in the case of suicide. Collins describes Schopenhauer's dissatisfaction with the alternative of suicide in the following way.

> If one approaches suicide in the somewhat quizzical spirit of wanting to find out what happens to human existence and knowledge after death, suicide entails the serious disadvantage of annihilating the individual inquirer himself. At death, the phenomenal individual is dissolved; all that remains unscathed is the single noumenal will, which is beyond all individual modes of being. If there is any human "immortality," it consists in acknowledging the truth of the proposition that only the cosmic will is everlasting. ....on the other hand, if one is driven by the burdens of existence to seek the termination of human misery, then suicide is not the proper method to use. For the death of the individual affects the will in no way, and leaves it in full possession of the field of experience. Hence, suicide fails to get at the root cause of the evils and sufferings of life. Indeed, suicide is a particularly strong affirmation of the will, rather than its radical negation. The suicide prizes the will-to-live so highly, that he destroys the individual obstacle to its fruition. He removes the frustrating conditions and, simultaneously, pays tribute to omnivorous will in all its power.[47]

Death by suicide or other means is merely the death of the individual; it is not the termination of the cosmic will. It still drives on dynamically and ruthlessly. But what is humankind's alternative; is there any decisive alternative that leads to releasement or liberation? Once again, Schopenhauer suggests the solution is indifference to the will. The will is the chain that binds us in the pain of struggle and suffering. If this chain can be broken, one can be free from the compulsions of life and lose oneself in quiet and serene contemplation. Human being is unique, not in its ability to will,for the will is cosmic; it is all encompassing. Human nature's uniqueness or "humanity is the only stage at which the will can deny itself, and completely turn away from life." Human being's uniqueness lies in its negation of the will through indifference and the serenity that ensues from aesthetic contemplation.

In turning to Nietzsche's philosophy of the will or his "Will zur Macht," the reader can find the logical conclusion of this

---

47. Collins. A History of Modern European Philosophy,p. 688.

tradition of volition. In Kant's ethics, the moral will was lifted to a position of absolute priority and primacy. The good moral will, according to Kant, was the only good in itself and also it was the apex of human knowing and activity. In Nietzsche's "Wille zur Macht," the culmination and logical conclusion of Kant's contentions can be discerned. The will, for Kant, was the supreme element or dimension of the self. The will under the regulation of practical reason lifts the human self from the existence of a mere thing to a transcendental existence. The will lifts one above appearance into the realm of "Things-in-Themselves." Nietzsche continues this deification of the will and contends that if the will is the primary reality, then it should seek to satisfy itself rather than subject itself to external criteria. For Kant, the will submitted itself to the scrutiny and regulation of reason. Reason was the key to the functioning of a "good moral will." If the will is prior ontologically, or if human nature is basically will and only secondarily rational, then why should the will subject itself to some facet or criteria other than itself? For Nietzsche, the will must and does justify itself and set its own criteria. The will, which was primary in Kant, reaches its full autonomy and significance in Nietzsche's view, the will wills for the sake of its own internal criteria and dynamics. In Also Sprach Zarathustra, Nietzsche describes the liberation of the will to its own demands in the following way:

> Verily, through a hundred souls I have already passed on my way, and through a hundred cradles and birth pangs. Many a farewell have I taken; I know the heart rending last hours. But thus my creative will, my destiny, wills it. Or, to say it more honestly: this very destiny--my will wills.
>
> Whatever in me has feeling, suffers and is in prison; but my will always comes to me as my liberator and joybringer. Willing liberates: that is the true teaching of will and liberty--thus Zarathustra teaches it. Willing no more and esteeming no more and creating no more--oh, that this great weariness might always remain far from me! In knowledge too I feel only my will's joy in begetting and becoming; and if there is innocence in my knowledge, it is because the will to beget is in it. Away from God and gods this will has lured me; what could one create if god existed?[48]

---

48. Kaufmann, Walter, The Portable Nietzsche, New York: Viking Press, 1968, p. 199.

The will is the key to the dynamic transformations that man is capable of affirming and enduring. The will can send us through a "hundred souls" and births if we have the courage to release it to itself and not seek to negate it or control others with it or to create gods and God with it. The will returns us radically and creatively to ourselves and to the vista of self transcendence which Nietzsche calls the "ubermensch." The will brings faithfulness to ourselves and to the earth:

> Behold, I teach you the overman. The overman is the meaning of the earth. Let your will say: The overman _shall_ be the meaning of the earth! I beseech you, my brothers, _remain faithful to the earth_, and do not believe those who speak to you of other worldly hopes! Poison-mixers are they, whether they know it or not. Despisers of life are they, decaying and poisoned themselves, of whom the earth is weary: so let them go.
>
> Once the sin against God was the greatest sin; but God died, and these sinners died with him. To sin against the earth is now the most dreadful thing, and to esteem the entails of the unknowable higher than the meaning of the earth.[49]

Humankind, in order to unleash the strength of its own creativity, must remain true to the earth. Instead of fleeing from the earth, oneself, and one's own awareness and creating another world, the individual, if he/she chooses the path of the "overman," must turn projections and imagination back on the self and its earth rather than alienating projections as a fabricated world which consciousness projects as separate from humankind. The "overman" does not rise above the world or earth and become a heavenly or spiritual being, but channels its creative energy upon itself and its earth.

Parallel and intrinsically related to Nietzsche's statements about the sins that humankind inflicts upon the earth are his contentions concerning the despisers of the body. For Nietzsche, human being is body--one does not have a body but is a body. The gods are merely projections about human creativity and likewise the soul is only a description of something about the body. "But the awakened and knowing say: body am I entirely and nothing else: and the soul is only a word for something about the body."[50] The body is your knowledge and knowing. Knowing and thought are

---

49. _Ibid._ p. 125.
50. _Ibid._ p. 146.

not a function of mind and spirit but are intrinsic to your body. "There is more reason in your body than in your best wisdom."[51] The body and the will are the ground and source of creativity and values. It is this that the despisers of the body fail to see. They try to crush the will and the body in order to enhance the spirit. Nietzsche counters their tendencies in the following way:

> I want to speak to the despisers of the body. It is their respect that begets their contempt. What is it that created respect and contempt and worth and will? The creative self created respect and contempt; it created pleasure and pain. The creative body created the spirit as a hand for its will.[52]

Despising the body is not the way of creativity. Negating the natural and the bodily is self-evasion. Only when the self seeks "to go under"; only when it can no longer transcend itself or meet its internal challenge for going beyond itself does it despise the body and seek to negate itself. "I shall not go your way, O despisers of the body! You are no bridge to the overman! Thus, spoke Zarathustra."[53] Only where and when I "will with all my will" there is myself and my creativity. Only where the will truly becomes its own "redeemer and joy bringer," only when the will seeks to satisfy its own demands, only then are we walking the tight rope to the overman. When the will that became prior and primary in Kant frees itself from reason and all other restraint, only then can it enhance itself in dynamic creativity and release the human self to itself.

Thus, the philosophical context which is the occasion for Nietzsche's philosophy of volition is deeply related, first of all, to the tradition of philosophy extending from Kant through Fichte, Schelling, and Schopenhauer. It grows out of a tradition which viewed the will as primary. It also assumes a distinctive form that is related to those philosophers of will in the 19th century, but is significantly distinct from them. This can be seen especially in Nietzsche's dependence on and opposition to Schopenhauer's theory of will.

Nietzsche discovered Schopenhauer during his first term of study at Leipzig in the fall of 1865. In his autobiographical writings from this era, the reader finds that Nietzsche came across

---

51. Ibid. p. 147

52. Ibid.

53. Ibid.

a copy of Schopenhauer's magnum opus in a second-hand bookshop. Nietzsche describes this experience in the following way:

> One day in old Rohn's second-hand bookshop, I came across this book, picked it up without knowing anything about it, and leafed through it. I don't know what demon whispered to me: 'Take it home.' I was certainly not in the habit of buying a book on the spur of the moment. At home, I threw myself into the corner of the sofa with my new treasure and gave myself up to that somber and forceful genius. Here, every line cried out renunciation, negation, resignation, here I saw a mirror reflecting the world, life, and my own heart and soul in horrifying grandeur.[54]

In Schopenhauer, Nietzsche confronted his first significant philosophical inspiration; an inspiration that was to lead Nietzsche to move from what he called the "neutral fields" of philosophy into the "palace of philosophy." Schopenhauer's influence on Nietzsche cannot be underestimated and it has been examined and explored at great length on many occasions by a variety of individuals. Wright, for example, sees the Schopenhauer experience to be tied deeply to Nietzsche's youthful enthusiasm. He describes Nietzsche's reaction to Schopenhauer's The World as Will and Idea in the following way:

> This book went far in arousing the philosophic faculties of the young philologist, and later he wrote many essays, long and short, both in praise and in refutation of the great pessimist. That he should at first have subscribed to all of Schopenhauer's teachings is natural. Nietzsche was vital and susceptible to enthusiasms. It was in accord with his youthful nature, full of courage and strength, that he should have been seduced to pessimism.[55]

---

54. Frenzel, Ivo. Friedrich Nietzsche, An Illustrated Biography, trans. by Joaquim Neugroschel, New York: Pegasus, 1967, p. 27. Frenzel is here quoting an early Nietzsche fragment.

55. Wright, Willard. What Nietzsche Taught, New York: B.W. Neubsche, 1917, p. 30-31.

For Wright, Schopenhauer appealed to Nietzsche's youthful pessimism and was one of Nietzsche's heroes in which he saw embodied the fearless "Freidenker" that he hoped to be. With Schopenhauer, Nietzsche agreed, in part, and saw the world as a grand dynamic arena in which only the blind and ruthless will prevailed. Nietzsche's dependence on Schopenhauer is seen to operate in different degrees. Brinton and Wolf argue that Nietzsche's pessimism was a youthful phase in his philosophy; a phase that he was eventually to react against and transform.[56] Kaufmann argues in much the same vein and also contends that Schopenhauer was important for Nietzsche's friendship with Wagner and the writing of The Birth of Tragedy, both of which fall in the early phases of Nietzsche's life and intellectual development. Paul Elmer More, in a short tract entitled Nietzsche, attaches far more significance to the relationship between Nietzsche and Schopenhauer's thought. More claims that all of Nietzsche's writings from The Birth of Tragedy to Zarathustra and The Will to Power are clearly the result of Schopenhauer's influence. More in this vein states:

> Rebel as he might in later years against Schopenhauer's pessimistic doctrine of blind, unmeaning will; try as he might to construct a positive doctrine out of that blank negation; he never got the poison out of his blood. Much of the pose and lyric misanthropy of Zarathustra is really an echo of what he read in his room on that fateful day.[57]

Whether or not it was a fateful day for Nietzsche when he discovered the philosophy of Schopenhauer is not the concern of this essay. It is also not crucial to decide, as does More, given his own petty problematics, whether or not Schopenhauer was a poison to Nietzsche's mind and life. What this author is concerned with is elucidating Nietzsche's relationship to philosophies of will and seeing Schopenhauer as crucial for Nietzsche's continuity with this tradition, but also his distinctive synthesis and culmination of the primary concerns of this tradition. It has been

---

56. Brinton, Crane. Nietzsche, Cambridge, Mass: Harvard University Press, 1941. Wolf, A. The Philosophy of Nietzsche, London: George Allen & Unwin Ltd., 1915.

57. More, Paul Elmer. Nietzsche. Boston and New York: Houghton Mifflin Co., 1912, pp. 8-9.

previously argued that Nietzsche's philosophy is the logical conclusion of Kant, Fichte, Schelling, and Schopenhauer's contentions concerning the primacy of will. At this point, the distinctive philosophy of will that Nietzsche develops will be explored. Up to this point, Nietzsche's continuity with the philosophical tradition that precedes him has been stressed and now Nietzsche's "Wille zur Macht" shall be explored on its own terms.

In the statements that have been discussed from Zarathustra, it is evident that Nietzsche proposes his theory of the will to power in opposition to those who negate life and the body. A distinction that is crucially associated with his ideas of life and body negation is the distinction between "active" and "passive" nihilism. In the first book of Nietzsche's Will to Power, one finds an elaborate description of the advent of nihilism, a description that will aid the reader in understanding the two forms of nihilism that have just been mentioned:

> What I relate is the history of the next two centuries. I describe what is coming, what can no longer come differently, the advent of nihilism. . . For some time now, our whole European culture has been moving as toward a catastrophe, with a tortured tension that is growing from decade to decade: restlessly, violently, headlong, like a river that wants to reach the end, that no longer reflects, that is afraid to reflect.[58]

The advent of nihilism occurs simultaneously with the demise of Christianity. Nietzsche sees three phases or stages in this demise. First of all, there occurred the weakening of Christianity and its plethora of beliefs and values. In response to this, western man ceased to be a Christian in the strict sense of the word, clung to and emphasized morality. Moral self replaced the religious self only temporarily, for soon it became evident that the values of moral humankind were a carry-over from the Christian faith. The demise of Christianity marked the end of humankind's judging this world on terms of a fabricated world of illusion. The problem in Nietzsche's worlds is acutely simple. "We have measured the value of the world according to categories that refer to a purely fictitious world."[59] The third stage that evolves when the illusion of the other world passes is the advent of nihilism. It is the view "that every belief, every considering-

---

58. Nietzsche, Friedrich, The Will to Power, ed. by Walter Kaufmann, New York: Randon House, 1968, p. 3.

59. Ibid. p. 13.

something-true, is necessarily false because there simply is no true world."[60] There are two forms that nihilism can take according to Nietzsche. The first is passive nihilism of weakness and negation of will. Schopenhauer, in Nietzsche's perspective, embodies the true form of passive nihilism. In Nietzsche's words, passive nihilism is "the weary nihilism that no longer attacks: its most famous form, Buddhism; a passive nihilism, a sign of weakness."[61] It is this kind of nihilism that Nietzsche sees operative in Schopenhauer. It is a nihilism and pessimism that leads to renunciation of self and world negation:

> Whoever has endeavored with some enigmatic longing, as I have, to think pessimism through to its depths and to liberate it from the half-Christian, half-German narrowness and simplicity in which it has finally presented itself to our century, namely in the form of Schopenhauer's philosophy; whoever has really, with an Asiatic and supra-Asiatic eye, looked into, down into the most world-denying of all possible ways of thinking -- beyond good and evil and no longer, like the Buddha and Schopenhauer, under the spell and delusion of morality -- may just thereby, without really meaning to do so, have opened his eyes to the opposite ideal: the ideal of the most high-spirited, alive, and world-affirming human being who has not only come to terms and learned to get along with whatever was and is.[62]

Passive nihilism in the Schopenhauerian form, for Nietzsche, merely marks an escape from nihilism. It is a "self-narcotization" and attempt to resign to nihilism and then hide from it. What results is an "un-egotistic," "self-denial," and "negation of the will."

For Nietzsche, Schopenhauer's nihilism seeks to annihilate the self in the same way as does Buddhism and Christianity.

> To what extent Schopenhauer's nihilism still follows from the same ideal that created Christian theism.--- One felt so certain about the highest desiderata, the

---

60. Ibid., p. 14.

61. Ibid., p. 18

62. Nietzsche, Friedrich. Beyond Good and Evil, trans. by Walter Kaufmann, New York: Random House, 1966, p. 68.

> highest values, the highest perfection that the philosophers assumed this as an absolute certainty, as if it were a priori: "God" at the apex as a given truth. For years these were the most naive and convincing desiderata (but what convinces is not necessarily true -- it is merely convincing: a note for asses.)[63]

Schopenhauer seeks to avoid and evade the will by absorption into aesthetic contemplation and artistic ideals. The Christian seeks to avoid himself through the cultivation of selflessness and ultimately through an absorption into Christ or God. Self evasion, finding its counterparts in Schopenhauer, Buddhism and a long history of Christianity has turned the humanself away from itself and into fear and weakness. It results in a negation of the creative dynamism of the will and ultimately turns man "into a sublime miscarriage."[64] Christianity seeks to make one sickly, weak,and "equal before God." Dynamic individualism is far too threatening for Christian sensibilities. In order to be truly Christian, one must be weak and humble; one must be like the "lamb of God."

Thus in Buddhism, Christianity, and the philosophy of Schopenhauer the key similarities are that each seeks to negate the will. Each of these also, according to Nietzsche, seeks to suppress the natural egotistic instincts of the self and the innate creative desire for dynamic individuality. Passive nihilism,similarly represented in each of these positions,turns one away from life, vitality, and will into the renunciation of self negation and

---

63. Nietzsche. The Will to Power, p. 15.

64. Nietzsche. Beyond Good and Evil, p. 75.

escapes into an undifferentiated state whether this be aesthetic release or absorption into the all or God.[65]

In contrast to Schopenhauer's passive nihilism, Nietzsche proposes an active nihilism. This form of nihilism is affirmative and rejoices in the realization that ultimate values are lacking. This form of nihilism affirms the will and cultivates its individual form and its ensuing personal freedom. Active nihilism is Nietzsche's understanding and actualization of the "will to power." As we have suggested via our interpretation of various passages from Zarathustra, the will to power is the liberation of the will to itself. The will turns to itself and exercises radical freedom and creative transformations. The will stimulates dynamic creativity which rejoices in itself and affirms life, the body, and the earth. The "will to power" is the self's way to the "ubermensch," the overman who distinguishes himself/herself in power and creativity. These rather volatile notions of freedom, power and creativity demand close attention and scrutiny because given their radical and volatile nature,they are vulnerable to gross and abortive misinterpretation.

---

65. Nietzsche connects Schopenhauer's negation of all will and Buddhism in the following way: (Nietzsche) On the Genealogy of Morals, ed., Walter Kaufmann, New York: Random House, 1969, p. 19.

> What was especially at stake was the value of the 'unegoistic,' the instincts of pity, self-abnegation, self-sacrifice, which Schopenhauer had gilded, deified, and projected into a beyond for so long that at last they became for him 'value-in-itself,' on the basis of which he said No to life and to himself. But it was against precisely these instincts that there spoke from me an ever more fundamental mistrust, an ever more corrosive skepticism! It was precisely here that I saw the great danger to mankind, its sublimist enticement and seduction--to what? to nothingness?--it was precisely here that I saw the beginning of the end, the dead stop, a retrospective weariness, the will turning against life, the tender and sorrowful signs of the ultimate illness: I understood the ever spreading morality of pity that had seized even on philosophers and made them ill, as the most sinister symptom of a European culture that had itself become sinister, perhaps as its by-pass to a new Buddhism? To a Buddhism for Europeans? to--nihilism?

Many of the misinterpretations of Nietzsche's understanding of the will to power stem out of the variety of ways in which Nietzsche treats the subject. In one of his essays on the origin and development of morality, that is, his work *On the Genealogy of Morals*, Nietzsche sees the will to power operative in the origin of moral differentiation. According to Nietzsche, moral distinctions and values arose out of the differentiation and conflict between the strong and the weak classes of people. The strong and the powerful acted as they saw fit and called what they did and were the good. They designated that which opposed them and ran counter to their desires as evil. In contrast to this, the person of mediocrity and weakness created his/her values through *ressentiment.* The noble self of strength and individuality "conceives the basic concept 'good' in advance and spontaneously out of himself/herself and only then creates for himself/herself and idea of 'bad!'"[66] Slave morality or the moral values of the weak classes are created "in the cauldron of unsatisfied hatred."[67] It is created through venomous hope for revenge and repressed hostility for those who,through their acts,become outstanding or separate and distinctive. Ultimately, says Nietzsche, the spirit of *ressentiment* becomes a democratization of the spirit. This leads to a leveling off and equalization of human values. Everyone must be similar; no one should be outstanding. Nietzsche sees this as a principle hostile to life and humankind. The democratic principle and the communistic theories to which it is analogous see self's essence in its commonness. Both contend: "that every will must consider every other will its equal -- would be a principle *hostile to life*, an agent of the dissolution and destruction of man, an attempt to assassinate the future of man, a sign of weariness, a secret path to nothingness.--"[68] This kind of equalization would reduce humankind to rabble and amorphous indifference. It would destroy those who excel and as a result destroy the possibility for excellence.

---

66. *Ibid.*, p. 39.

67. *Ibid.*, p. 40.

68. *Ibid.*, p. 76

Even though the struggle for power and the subjection of lower classes to the will of higher and more powerful classes is a manifestation of the "will to power," Nietzsche far from approves of this tendency in all of its varying forms. Walter Kaufmann clarifies Nietzsche's contention concerning the "will to power" in the following way:

> It is thus apparent that Nietzsche approached the conception of a will to power from two fairly distinct points of view. First, he thought of it as a craving for worldly success which he repudiated as harmful to man's interest in perfecting himself. Secondly, he thought of the will to power as a psychological drive in terms of which many diverse phenomena could be explained, e.g., gratitude, pity, and self-abasement. The phrase "will to power" is not yet used, except in one note, and Nietzsche far from approves of this urge. While one cannot, on the basis of the evidence so far considered, make any sweeping statements about Nietzsche's philosophy, it seems worth insisting that, at least at first, Nietzsche used the will to power as a principle to explain behavior and did not picture it as a virtue. In fact, he used it generally to explain behavior which he happened to dislike. He did not exhort people to develop a will to power, nor did he speak of it as anything glorious.[69]

A particular form of the "will to power" that Nietzsche opposed and the form concerning which he was most brutally misrepresented was political power and the power of states. The Nazi's use of Nietzsche's works was the most blatant of these brutal travesties. The Nazi editors were very careful in their selection of Nietzsche's works and aphorisms. The Nazis systematically avoided Nietzsche's statements concerning the desirability of a "European League of Nations." They also omitted Nietzsche's statements concerning European culture and his frequent sneers at the German people. They also forgot that,as a student,Nietzsche joined a fraternity that specialized in beer drinking, dueling, and nationalism. Nitzsche was repulsed by all three of these primary activities and tried to reform the fraternity with intellectual discussion, failed,and left the fraternity after a matter of days. Most blatant of all the statements the Nazis avoided were Nietzsche's contentions concerning peace, a peace based on total disarmament.

---

69. Kaufmann, Walter. Nietzsche, Cleveland and New York: The World Publishing Co., 1966, p. 159.

Nietzsche sees this as the only

> means to real peace, which must always rest on a peace of mind; whereas the so-called armed peace, as it now exists in all countries, is the absence of peace of mind. One trusts neither oneself nor one's neighbor and, half from hatred, half from fear, does not lay down arms. Rather perish than hate and fear, and <u>twice rather perish than make oneself hated and feared</u> -- this must someday become the highest maxim for every single commonwealth too.[70]

Kaufmann summarizes Nietzsche's dissatisfaction with political and national power, focusing it on the German Reich in the following manner:

> The might of the German <u>Reich</u> does not impress Neitzsche. To bow before such strength is slavish. One might expect Nietzsche to base his repudiation on the assertion that only a weak nation finds it necessary to impress itself and others with barbarian brawn and armies, and that culture is a higher, i.e., a quantitatively greater, form of power.... This repudiation of power as an evil principle becomes explicit in Nietzsche's denunciation of the German <u>Reich</u>. It is repudiated not because brawn is a manifestation of small power, but because power is a demon.... Neitzsche is looking upon the German <u>Reich</u> of Bismark, upon a nation thrilled by its love of power, upon a people willing to risk their bodies, their gods, and their children in war, a people who would "let go" even their "honor" -- for the sake of the Reich. "Yes! Yes! The 'Reich'!"[71]

Kaufmann sees Nietzsche's statement as prophetic rather than affirmative. Nietzsche realized that the kind of nationalization pervasive in the culture of his time could give way to the most atrocious allegiances and duties. The historical actualization of Nietzsche's prophecies are so acutely present in our memories and history that they need not be mentioned. The Nazis who claimed Nietzsche as their seer decisively demonstrated that what Nietzsche feared could and did come true.

---

70. <u>Ibid</u>., p. 161.

71. Ibid., p. 170-1.

Much of the misuse and confusion in interpretation of Nietzsche's "will to power" stems from the word power. The German Macht is consistently translated as power and this translation leads us into confusing nuances and associations. Power in English connotes power over other individuals. When we think of power and powerful individuals we tend to think of powerful political figures. This, however, is not what Nietzsche intended and meant by this word. The highest and most genuine form of the "will to power," the form promoted and affirmed by *Zarathustra*, is the will to self-transcendence. Self-transcendence is the self going beyond itself, not a person seeking to subdue his fellow human beings. The "ubermensch" distinguishes himself/herself through outstanding creativity and not through his control and subjugation of others. It seems, then, that the word power is misleading, for it connotes control and subjugation. If the reader looks for another translation of the word Macht, one finds that potency is a valid translation of this word. The question thus becomes whether "potency" is a valid interpretation of Nietzsche's meaning and views?

Our first clue lies in the word Ohnmacht, which Nietzsche uses to describe the opposite of the "Wille zur Macht."[72] Ohnmacht is impotence in its most direct meaning. It also suggests dependence, fear, and powerlessness. Thus, Macht as Ohnmacht's opposite, is creative potency in the broadly metaphorical sense: neither restricted to the Aristotelian potency (which largely refers to potential) nor restricted to the sexual meaning (which implies sexual inadequacy). By a broad metaphorical use of this word it is suggested that potency can be used as a metaphor that encompasses all of man's creative and dynamically positive actions. The "Wille zur Macht" would be the will to creative potency or the will to dynamic self-energization. Thus Macht, rather than meaning power over other individuals, would suggest the release of individual energies which are vital to self-actualization and self-transformation. Macht, rather than connotating political power, would refer to the actualization of energies intrinsic and necessary to a creative internal politics of the self. Macht, rather than implying national power or power that the strong use to enslave others, would be a power of potency unleashed for the sake of individual creativity and strength. Thus, potency used as a broad metaphor encompassing the entire spectrum of human creativity, more adequately describes the drive to individual creativity that Nietzsche implies in his concept of the "Wille zur Macht." To validate this we must try to verify the contention that creativity was the goal to which Nietzsche directed his concept of Macht.

---

72. *Ibid.*, p. 159.

Nietzsche does not speak often of the good or a supreme locus of values in the positive sense. The reason for this is that he seeks to lift the imagination beyond good and evil in its search for novel ways of appreciating and interpreting the world and human life. The reader finds a passage in the "Wille zur Macht" that speaks to the present concerns and is indicative of Nietzsche's affirmation of individual creativity. Here Nietzsche directly states what he views as the good. "There is nothing better than what is good -- and good is having some ability and using that to create..."[73] To create thus becomes the highest act of humankind. To create becomes the highest and most sublime expression of the will. Energies that in former eras and other situations were used to control and enslave peoples and nations are now, in Nietzsche's perspective, best used to unravel the self and to unleash creativity. Hostile energies explosively released on war and combat now become the energy for the internal dialectics of self-interpretation. Power and control are directed and focused on the creativity of the self. In discussing "what is noble," Nietzsche contends the following concerning power and the self:

> The noble human being honors himself as one who is powerful, also as one who has power over himself, who knows how to speak and be silent, who delights in being severe and hard with himself and respects all severity and hardness.[74]

Power and control are directed internally. Energy is channeled back towards the self so that its creativity can be explored and exploited. The "will to power" becomes the will to dynamic potency and creative self-knowledge.

Karl Jaspers, in his work Nietzsche, describes and interprets the "will to power" as a "new exegesis."[74] Exegesis in this meaning is humankind's relationship with itself. The basic focus

---

73. Nietzsche. The Will to Power, p. 48.

74. Nietzsche. Beyond Good and Evil, p. 205.

75. Jaspers, Karl. Nietzsche, Tucson: The University of Arizona Press, 1965.

for knowledge is self-interpretation. Jaspers uses the word exegesis as a metaphor to encompass humankind's interpretive turn towards itself and being:

> The metaphor of "exegesis," used to express the basic relation of human existence to being, is taken by Nietzsche from the relation of interpretation to text in philological work. The text contains a meaning which the interpretation is intended to discover. What is given as factual and unalterable is the text or, in another sense, a meaning to be conveyed by it, which may or may not be properly understood; and an interpretation that goes beyond this is open to question. It is the business of philology to approach the true meaning of old texts by eliminating premature, wildly imaginative, and inventive renderings. In dealing with literary documents, philology expresses its newly won understanding; thus in understanding texts, it creates new texts. The unique movement and dialectic of philological understanding provides Nietzsche with a metaphor suitable for expressing the understanding of being on the part of the existence that construes it.[76]

Interpretation serves to unravel and unleash the hidden text of the self and its latent creativity. Interpretation of self exegesis does not pretend to give us knowledge of the world as a whole. Interpretation seeks to unravel and subtly unlock humankind's creativity and potency. Jaspers, in quoting and paraphrasing Nietzsche on this issue, says the following:

> Nietzsche warns us against <u>all</u> notions of the whole: "Let us guard against thinking that the world is a living being . . . or that the universe is a machine . . . .Let us guard against saying that there are laws of nature ... Let us guard against thinking that the world eternally creates novelties." All these "shadows of God" darken actuality. We are within the world, and the whole of the world is, <u>as a whole</u>, not accessible to us.[77]

The alternative then, is to turn to the self and to individuality and the distinctive personal will. The world as a whole may not be open for humankind's penetrating insight, but consciousness gives rise to the possibility of interpretation and

---

76. <u>Ibid</u>., p. 289.

77. <u>Ibid</u>., p. 293.

introspective awareness. This form of interpretation and introspective exegesis is radically historical and decisively individual. It is opposed to any fixed absolute or eternal position and turns to the "point where I myself as a unique and inimitable individual must, in truth, read (i.e., construe) being, since I am as I am." The "*Wille zur Macht*" thus is "experienced as the truth of *Existenz* itself."[78] The exegetical knower lives in the fullness of "historical consciousness" and in fullness of a self that releases itself to itself through willing its fullest potency. As a result, in each historical moment the truth of existence is present in the immediacy of the creative and potent self. Each moment and each manifestation of historical consciousness has within it the potential for the fullness of life and truth. In each moment, if the will is released to its optimal expression in creativity, the fullness of being or creative individuality presses human consciousness into a potent self awareness that eternally recurs. The individual affirms himself/herself in an eternal "Yes" to the radically finite and acutely historical and "eternally recurring" will and its fertile field, the moment.

---

78. *Ibid*., p. 291.

ESSAY III:

CREATIVITY AND TIME

Nietzsche's theory of time is an essential facet of his theory of creativity. Nietzsche re-evaluates values and destroys cultural idols,but retains an uncompromising affirmation of human creativity. Human creation redeems life and culture. It is the only occasion in which a human being creates eternity.

In Zarathustra, the fourth part, Nietzsche describes his theory of creativity and time. He asks his reader:

> Have you ever said yes to a single joy? Oh my friends then you said yes too to all woe. All things are entangled, ensnared, enamored; if ever you wanted one thing twice, if ever you said, 'You please me, happiness! Abide, moment!' then you wanted all back. All anew, all eternally, all entangled, ensnared, enamored--oh then you loved the world. Eternal ones, love it eternally and evermore; and woe too, you say: go but return! For all joy wants--eternity.[1]

Willing the eternity of all things is to affirm the eternal recurrence. To experience one moment of sublime fullness, to create and contribute to the richness of nature and culture is for the experience of the few, the rare, the individual.

In the moment absolute finitude is both present and redeemed. Radical temporality is transformed through affirmation into eternity. If this is possible, then humankind can by themselves give value to their entire lives, transform their suffering, and justify their existence.

Time is essential to affirmation. Nietzsche pondered the concept of eternal return as recurrence and thought that it followed from the laws of conservation of matter and energy.[2] The specific source that appears to have deeply affected Nietzsche's thoughts on eternal recurrence was Heinrich Heine:

---

1. Friedrich Nietzsche, The Portable Nietzsche, Edited and translated by Walter Kaufmann (New York: The Viking Press, 1968), p. 435.

2. The Will to Power, Edited and translated by Walter Kaufmann, (New York: Vintage Books, 1967), p. 547, Nietzsche states, "The law of the conservation of energy demands eternal recurrence."

> ...And she answered with a tender voice: 'Let us be good friends,'--But what I have told you here, dear reader, that is not an event of yesterday or the day before... For time is infinite, but the things in time, the concrete bodies, are finite. They may indeed disperse into the smallest particles; but these particles, the atoms, have their determinate number, and the number of configurations which, all of themselves, are formed out of them is also determinate. Now, however long a time may pass, according to the eternal laws governing the combinations of this eternal play of repetition, all configurations which have previously existed on this earth must yet meet, attract, repulse, kiss, and corrupt each other again... And thus it will happen one day that a man will be born again, just like me, and a woman will be born, just like Mary--only that it is to be hoped that the head of this man may contain a little less foolishness--and in a better land they will meet and contemplate each other a long time; and finally the woman will give her hand to the man and say with a tender voice: 'Let us be good friends.'[3]

Time for Nietzsche is infinite. The physical objects and particles that exist in space are,however,finite. In addition,the possible forms of configuration and combination are likewise finite. Thus in infinite time all possible combinations occur and must be repeated. Nietzsche's statement of the issue is similar to Heine's:

> The sum-total of energy is limited not 'boundless' - let us beware of similar exaggeration in these concepts! It follows that the number of states, combinations, changes and transformations is tremendously great and practically immeasurable yet in any case finite and not infinite. Indeed the time in which the sum total of energy is active is infinite which implies that Energy is eternally similar and eternally active. Up to this moment an eternity has already run its course which means that all possible transformations must have already occurred.[4]

---

3. Heinrich Heine, Sämtliche Werke, Edited by Elster, Vol.III, p. 542, as translated by Walter Kaufmann in Nietzsche (New York: Meridian Books, 1966), p. 273.

4. Friedrich Nietzsche, Sämtliche Werke, Vol. XI, Part II, "Zu Zarathustra," p. 463, Translation mine.

Eternal return and recurrence of the same occurs. The infinity of time dictates that this occurs not once or twice but innumerable times.

Nietzsche is particularly interested in the psychological and existential effects and response of individuals to this concept. He poses the concept as an "as if" or a "what if" or in an awkward but correct translation, "how if:"

> The greatest stress. How, if some day or night a demon were to sneak after you into your loneliest loneliness and say to you, 'This life as you now live it and have lived it, you will have to live once more and innumerable times more; and there will be nothing new in it, but every pain and every joy and every thought and sigh and everything immeasurably small or great in your life must return to you--all in the same succession and sequence--even this spider and this moonlight between the trees, and even this moment and I myself. The eternal hourglass of existence is turned over and over, and you with it, a dust grain of dust.' Would you not throw yourself down and gnash your teeth and curse the demon who spoke thus? Or did you once experience a tremendous moment when you would have answered him, 'You are a god, and never have I heard anything more godly.' If this thought were to gain possession of you, it would change you, as you are, or perhaps crush you. The question in each and every thing, 'Do you want this once more and innumerable times more?' would weigh upon your actions as the greatest stress. Or how well disposed would you have to become to yourself and to life to crave nothing more fervently than this ultimate eternal confirmation and seal?[5]

For Nietzsche this is the supreme test of human existence. If one could joyously affirm the absolute repeatability of all things, i.e., the return and eternal return of all the movements of one's existence then the individual had sealed into his or her existence, an affirmation,a "yes" that transforms all pain, boredom,and triviality into significance through a moment that defies time and lives on in infinity. As Walter Kaufmann states it:

---

5. Nietzsche, The Portable Nietzsche, pp. 101-102.

> This is the apotheosis of the suprahistorical outlook, the supreme exaltation of the moment. Negatively, the doctrine of eternal recurrence is the most extreme repudiation of any depreciation of the moment, the finite and the individual--the antithesis of any faith which pins its hopes on infinite progress whether it be evolution, Faust's unbounded striving or the endless improvement of the human soul in Kant's conception of immortality. It is the antithesis, too, of any faith which looks to another world; it is the creed of one whose message began: 'I beseech you my brothers, remain faithful to the earth and do not believe those who speak to you of other worldly hopes.'[6]

For Nietzsche the individual and all acts and responses within the human condition can be justified from within human life itself. External transcendental justification is sheer escapism and stems from the attempt to foster human weakness and dependency rather than affirm creativity and strength. Transcending oneself and setting immeasurable high ideals for the self was the only transcendence Nietzsche would celebrate. It too was illusory but it did not lead humankind away from itself but turned human beings to the task of becoming their own creators and redeemers rather than looking for a "divine" figure or movement to offer them salvation.

Nietzsche's view of time and creativity contains the paradox of simultaneously assuming both freedom and determinism. If all events return and recur then what occurs has already occurred innumerable times before and thus human affirmation represents an acceptance of the infinite past and an infinite future. The choice lies only in rejoicing and affirmation or if the response is negative then the result is an exercise in futility or despair. Nietzsche's position appears to resemble the Stoics in that fate and freedom are reconciled. The Stoics believed that all circumstance was determined by fate. Human freedom resided in the responses made to external pressures and possibilities. Humankind for Nietzsche could defy the absurdity of eternal recurrence by excelling in acts of creation. Each act carried with it a connotation that we treat it "as if" it were our free uncompromising choice and "as if" it determined the course of our life for all eternity.

Nietzsche sought ideas and ideals that would exact from humankind the greatest intellectual and psychological courage.

---

6. Ibid., p. 125.

Human beings, if they were capable of self transcendence, can live with conscious illusion instead of losing themselves and their identity in belief in their ideals. The tendency is to be lost and overwhelmed by illusions and so-called tricks. Nietzsche sought to critically expose naive faiths as they posited the ultimate goodness and justifiability of all things. He also opposed nihilism that moved passively and resignedly to the lethargy of declaring anything and everything absurd. Creators of value and aesthetic form could turn to the moment and bring to it the joy of eternity.

Another way in which freedom and determination play a significant role for Nietzsche's concept of creativity and time focuses on the will. The will seeks freedom from that which is determined. The most significant vista that defies change is the past. In Zarathustra II, in the section on "Redemption," the relationship between the will and the past is described as follows:

> Because there is suffering in those who will, inasmuch as they cannot will backwards, willing itself and all life were supposed to be--a punishment. And now cloud upon cloud rolled over the spirit, until eventually madness preached, 'Everything passes away; therefore everything deserves to pass away. And this too is justice, this law of time that it must devour its children.' Thus preached madness.[7]

For Nietzsche the will can become its own "liberator and joy-bringer." It can redeem existence through becoming a creator. The will does not accept the "it was" of the past as normative for the present. A form of freedom from the past is the overcoming of revenge. Being hostile and angry about the past or any moment in it leads to attempts to seek revenge for it. The past like all things must and does perish. One must freely let the present end, perceiving its finitude. Revenge seeks to reverse the past, and analogous to resentment it assigns significance to a value or an act external to the will. What I can not and do not will is not me. Here Nietzsche once again resembles the Stoics. Freedom may not be complete. What there is of freedom is finite and limited, but its significance is absolute and its results eternal.

Joan Stambaugh in her excellent book on Nietzsche maintains that finitude "means impermanence." Eternal return through repetition "gives permanence to Becoming, in the sense that the

---

7. Ibid., p. 252.

Same recurs again and again, thus constituting a kind of interrupted, periodically recurring duration."[8] This odd accidental continuity provides a stability to be transcended. The will must transcend its own moments of accomplishment. The will does not merely strive for chaos and flux. It strives to impose "Being on Becoming." It can and does celebrate chaos, absurdity, and nihilism, but it seeks to transcend them and not become a victim or object of them. The will does not depend on or seek the guarantees of permanence. It seeks meaning through the creation of significance. The will seeks no eternal assurance. It seals the present as the end of one's acts.

The will does not desire to create "more" for the sake of improvement. If it does not will more it ceases to be will for its own past has closed its possibilities. Life for Nietzsche is possibility. It is richness and form. It is power (Macht), i.e., creative potency. Thinking should contribute to the fullness and complexity of life. One's view of time should be a celebration of the vastness but finitude of form and the infinite and eternal recurrence of the same. Freedom and determinism are brought together in the moment. Likewise time and elements, the finite and the infinite, are woven and entangled in the paradox of utter temporality and the creation of eternity. The will wills forward, not backward. It does not allow itself the pessimistic ease of living mechanically-repetitiously and resignedly to what was. The only future is a willfully created future.

Fate for Nietzsche is not outside oneself. Humankind is not against the world or the Universe but is a part of it. Human beings do not attain their creative powers by gaining distance from nature. Nietzsche makes this view clear in the following passages:

> The whole attitude of 'man versus the world,' as world-denying principle, man as the standard of the value of things, as judge of the world, who in the end puts existence itself on his scales and finds it too light--the monstrous impertinence of this attitude has dawned upon us as such, and has disgusted us; we now laugh when we find 'Man and World' placed beside one another,

---

8. Joan Stambaugh, Nietzsche's Thought of Eternal Return, (Baltimore and London: The Johns Hopkins University Press, 1972), p. 13.

separated by the submlime presumption of the little word 'and!'[9]

Turkish fatalism. Turkish fatalism contains the fundamental error of placing man and fate opposite each other like two separate things: Man, it says, can strive against fate, can try to defeat it, but in the end it always remains the winner, for which reason the smartest thing to do is to give up or live just any way at all. The truth is that every man himself is a piece of fate; when he thinks he is striving against fate in the way described, fate is being realized here, too; the struggle is imaginary, but so is resignation to fate; all these imaginary ideas are included in fate. The fear which most people have of the doctrine of determinism of the will is precisely the fear of this Turkish fatalism. They think man will give up weakly and stand before the future with folded hands because he cannot change anything about it; or else he will give free rein to his total caprice because even this cannot make what is once determined still worse. The follies of man are just as much a part of fate as his cleverness: this fear of the belief in fate is also fate. You, yourself, poor frightened man, are the invincible Moira reigning far above the gods; for everything which comes, you are blessing or curse and in any case the bonds in which the strongest man lies. In you the whole future of the human world is predetermined; it will not help you if you are terrified of yourself.[10]

If all things are determined then human beings are an active dimension of that determination. Nature and humankind are caught in the self same nexus of freedom and determinism. The cauldron in which both are stirred is the moment.

Fate for Nietzsche was not something to despise and curse. The fallacy of resignation resided in presuming that fate exists outside of the human dimension. Freedom is occasioned through a

---

9. Friedrich Nietzsche, The Gay Science, translation by Walter Kaufmann (New York: Vintage Books, 1974), pp. 286-287.

10. Nietzsche, The Wanderer and His Shadow, 61 as translated by Stambaugh in Nietzsche's Thought of Eternal Return, p. 57.

love of fate amor fati or, as Joan Stambaugh states it, "the identity of the highest fatalism with the Creative."[11]

Nietzsche rejects the simple and easy thoughts concerning eternal recurrence. As a thought Nietzsche pursues its most difficult and demanding form. The simple resignation of endless repetition demands nothing of humankind but cowardice and acquiescence. One is what one is. To resign oneself is to presume that the force of fate is external to the self. One lives fate and is fate. Eternal recurrence is a thought concerning time and creativity within those processes. It is a moment a Versuch, i.e., an experiment. It is however neither arbitrary nor purely subjective. As Joan Stambaugh succinctly states it:

> No matter what interpretation is given to eternal recurrence, it always remains a thought, for Nietzsche thought it, and whoever reads him is also presumably thinking about it. Even the 'factual' emphasis of the first interpretation is basically just another way of thinking eternal recurrence. This is not to say that it is something 'subjective.' There is nothing arbitrary or subjective about Nietzsche's thought. The whole basis for such arbitrariness is lacking in his philosophy. On the other hand, his thought is not subject to a kind of 'determinism,' a complete subjection of the human being to some inscrutable mechanism of fate. Nietzsche's concern lies not in the subjection of man to fate but in man's relation to that fate. It makes no sense for man to prostrate himself on the ground before fate, because he, himself, belongs to, is that fate. To prostrate oneself before oneself is comic.[12]

Neither Humankind nor nature are either completely free or completely determined. Both are capable of novelty, richness and complexity. Both have the continuity of similar form. Absolute originality would destroy any continuity or coherence. The moment exists in part in the return of the same and the free selection of a future. Chance, freedom, and creativity meet in the finitude and infinity of the moment. As Nietzsche states this cryptically, "Highest fatalism, but identical with chance and the Creative (No repetition in things, this must first be created)."[13]

---

11. Stambaugh, Nietzsche's Thought of Eternal Return, p. 56.

12. Ibid.

13. Nietzsche, Nachlass, XIV: 99 as translated in Stambaugh, Nietzsche's Thought of Eternal Recurrence, p. 59.

Nietzsche promotes what he refers to as active nihilism. The eternal return and the paradox of the radically temporal being eternal in its repetition of forms,may be the heaviest thought, but the beauty of human power and creativity is that it can celebrate this thought and not resign itself to weakness and despair. Nietzsche makes it clear in the collection of fragments known as the Will to Power that he opposes a passive nihilism. Nihilism for Nietzsche was in a "pathological, transitional stage."[14] It could be transformed, however, through the power of the idea of eternal recurrence. Nietzsche asks his reader to do the following: "Let us think this thought in its most terrible form without meaning and aim yet recurring inevitably without any finale of nothingness: 'the eternal recurrence.'"[15] Nietzsche favors pressing thought in a Heraclitean fashion to its most extreme form until it became transformed and affirms life. Traits, e.g., that were taken to be cruel and barbarous, Nietzsche thought might well harbor strength and potential creativity. This is one of the reasons Nietzsche was so vehemently critical of morality. Morality "teaches men to hate and despise most profoundly what is the basic character trait of those who rule: their will to power. To abolish, deny, and dissolve this morality--that would mean looking at the best-hated drive with an opposite feeling and valuation."[16] Nietzsche does not affirm all forms of the will to power, but seeks those forms that turn human beings upon themselves to exact from themselves a transformation of life and culture. This is active nihilism. It does not seek escape or nirvana. It desires only the power and the transformation of the act of human creation.

Nietzsche's celebration of the Moment is not the "remain moment thou art so beautiful" of Goethe's Faust. Faust sought the moment of perfect satiation through magic and power over time and the lives of others. Nietzsche seeks the moment through the creative act, i.e., through art, through the aphorism and through power over ourselves. Philosophy is for Nietzsche one of the highest and most beautiful forms. To reduce all of reality to an insight, although Nietzsche repeatedly argues against this as erroneous, is an expression of the most profound creative power. He says, "philosophy is this tyrannic urge itself, is the most spiritual will to power."[17] Art stems from the same source and serves similar purposes. "What is essential in art remains its

---

14. Nietzsche, The Will to Power, p. 14.

15. Ibid., pp. 36-37.

16. Nietzsche, The Gay Science, p. 351.

17. Friedrich Nietzsche, Beyond Good and Evil, translation by Walter Kaufmann (New York: The Viking Press, 1966), p. 16.

perfection of existence, its production of perfection and plenitude; art is essentially affirmation, blessing deification of existence." Art is viewed by Nietzsche as an extremely broad category, art is a manifestation of life; it is "The world as a work of art that gives birth to itself."[18] There is no separation of art from the world or of humankind in creativity from either. A human life well lived is an art work. A self that transforms itself and existence in its creative acts is reflective of the dynamism of the world of nature.

Goethe's life was a model for Nietzsche: "In Goethe a kind of almost joyous and trusting fatalism that does not revolt, that does not flag, that seeks to form a totality out of himself, in the faith that only in the totality everything redeems itself and appears good and justified."[19] Goethe found pleasure in life. He created. He lived a celebration of excellence. He took to perennial themes of myth and literature and gave them novelty and creative form. His life was an affirmation of life itself.

For Nietzsche life is not separate from thought. The two can be separated but then both lose vitality and significance. Thought and life are the fusion of freedom and form. They are the temporary limitation of vast possibilities into significant structure and coherence. Nietzsche's philosophy can be erroneously interpreted as a celebration of chaos. It is rather an affirmation of the joy that chaos can be fused with form, the Apollonian joined to the Dionysian, and that both the highest and deepest forms of nihilism can be transcended.

Nietzsche, like Goethe, did not think that form was subjective, arbitrary,or superficial. Intellectual structures and patterns of coherence did not, however, grasp the essence of things. First of all, according to Nietzsche, there may be no essence of things. There may be no "real world." Truth is a fiction built upon illusion of essences and reality. Nature for Goethe was a great _Geheimnis_, a secret of which we come to know just a very little. This is not to say that we know nothing of nature. We know nature as phenomena. We know nature through ourselves. As Goethe states it: "Does not the key to nature lie within the

---

18. Nietzsche, _The Will to Power_, p.692.

19. _Ibid._, p. 796.

heart of man?"[20] Nietzsche promotes a similar viewpoint in a poem dedicated to Goethe:

> World game, the ruling force,
> blends false and true:
> the eternally fooling force
> blends us in too.[21]

The life and logic of nature is expressed in human thought as well as other forms and moments of nature.

For Neitzsche and Goethe there is continuity between human thought and other natural phenomena. Thought does not absolutely know or represent nature; it, however, reflects the whole of which it is a part. In this respect the thinking of Nietzsche and Goethe resembles that of William James. Thinking is a facet of nature.

> Philosophies are intimate parts of the universe;... A philosophy may indeed be a most momentous reaction of the universe upon itself... Our philosophies swell the current of being, add their character to it.[22]

Nietzsche's position on the indistinguishability of mind and body is linked with his theory of reason. Reason, for example, for Nietzsche is not merely a function of Mind. He states:

> I want to speak to the despisers of the body. I would not have them learn and teach differently, but merely say farewell to their own bodies--and thus become silent.
>
> 'Body am I, and soul'--thus speaks the child. And why should one not speak like children?
>
> But the awakened and knowing say: body am I entirely, and nothing else; and soul is only a word for something about the body.

---

20. In the beginning of Chapter XVIII, "On the Possibility of Knowing the Thing in Itself," Schopenhauer quotes this line from Goethe's poetry.

21. Nietzsche, The Gay Science, "The Songs of Prince Vogelfrei," p. 351.

22. William James, A Pluralistic Universe (Cambridge: Harvard University Press, 1977), p. 143.

> The body is a great reason, a plurality with one sense, a war and a peace, a herd and a shepherd. An instrument of your body is also your little reason, my brother, which you call 'spirit'--a little instrument and toy of your great reason.[23]

For Nietzsche "there is more reason in your body than in your best wisdom."[24] The body is the creator whereas the "will" and the "spirit" are devices and tools for the body.

The despisers of the body adhere to the dualism that denegrates the body because they are incapable of creativity. They devise the "other worldly" to give themselves sources and targets of significance. The despisers of the body turn away from life and creativity:

> Even in your folly and contempt, you despisers of the body, you serve your self. I say unto you: your self itself wants to die and turns away from life. It is no longer capable of what it would do above all else: to create beyond itself. That is what it would do above all else, that is its fervent wish.
>
> But now it is too late for it to do this: so your self wants to go under, O despisers of the body. Your self wants to go under, and that is why you have become despisers of the body! For you are no longer able to create beyond yourselves.[25]

Nature, mind, and body are all linked for Nietzsche through moments of creativity and volition. Life and thought do not need to turn away from themselves. Creativity for Nietzsche is a celebration of the earth, the body, and the creative will. Time, volition, and human existence are fused in the act of creation and its arena, the moment. Time and creativity assume significance because of each other and the influence they have on the life of the individual.

---

23. Nietzsche, Zarathustra in The Portable Nietzsche, p. 146.

24. Ibid.

25. Ibid., p. 147.